MEASURING THE EFFECTIVENESS OF SOUND PICTURES AS TEACHING AIDS

BY

VARNEY C. ARNSPIGER, Ph.D.

TEACHERS COLLEGE, COLUMBIA UNIVERSITY
CONTRIBUTIONS TO EDUCATION, NO. 565
Professor George D. Strayer, Sponsor

BUREAU OF PUBLICATIONS
Teachers College, Columbia University
NEW YORK CITY
1933

Library of Congress Cataloging in Publication Data

Arnspiger, Varney Clyde, 1896-
  Measuring the effectiveness of sound pictures as
teaching aids.

  Reprint of the 1933 ed., issued in series: Teachers
College, Columbia University. Contributions to educa-
tion, no. 565.
  Originally presented as the author's thesis, Columbia.
  Includes bibliographies.
  1. Moving-pictures in education. 2. Natural history
--Study and teaching--Audio-visual aids. 3. Music--
Instruction and study--Audio-visual aids. I. Title.
II. Series: Columbia University. Teachers College.

Contributions to education, no. 565.
LB1044.A73 1972   371.33'522   71-176524
ISBN 0-404-55565-9

Reprinted by Special Arrangement with Teachers
College Press, New York, New York

From the edition of 1933, New York
First AMS edition published in 1972
Manufactured in the United States

AMS PRESS, INC.
NEW YORK, N. Y.   10003

Columbia University

Contributions to Education

Teachers College Series

No. 565

AMS PRESS

NEW YORK

ACKNOWLEDGMENTS

THE author wishes to express his appreciation for the guidance and assistance of his sponsor, Professor George D. Strayer, and the valuable contributions of his dissertation committee, Professors Paul R. Mort, James R. McGaughy, and Peter W. Dykema. To Professor N. L. Engelhardt, Superintendent A. J. Stoddard, and Mr. H. G. Stokes, the writer is deeply indebted for constructive suggestions regarding the administration of the experiment. Grateful acknowledgment is due to the superintendents, supervisors, principals, and teachers of the cities participating in the experiment. Without their wholehearted cooperation and professional assistance the study would not have been possible. The author wishes to thank Dr. Frederick L. Devereux of Erpi Picture Consultants, Inc., for the use of the films and supplementary teaching materials which were prepared by the research and production staffs of this organization. Assistance in the construction of tests, in the field supervision of the experiment and in the tabulation of results by the writer's associates, Dr. Laura Krieger Eads, Dr. Howard A. Gray, Mr. James A. Brill, Dr. Melvin A. Brodshaug, Mr. Edgar M. Stover, and Dr. Max R. Brunstetter was invaluable. To his wife, Fay King Arnspiger, the author is indebted for sympathetic criticism and encouragement.

V. C. A.

CONTENTS

CHAPTER   PAGE

I. INTRODUCTION 1
    Historical Background 1
      The Middlesex Experiment 1
      Fox Film Experiment 3
      Experiment by Dr. C. C. Clark 4
      Erpi Experiment in Teacher Training 7
    The Problem of This Study 9

II. DESCRIPTION OF EXPERIMENT 10
    Scope of the Study 10
    The Technique Followed 10
    The Educational Sound Pictures Used 11
    Types of Subject Matter Tests 11
    Preliminary Testing 12
    Scoring the Tests 13
    Reliability of the Tests 13
    Selection of Cities Participating in the Experiment . . . 14
    Selection of Individual Classes and Teachers 14
    Results of Intelligence Test 15
    Results of Initial Tests 16
    Teaching Procedure and Time Allotments 19
    The Unit of Instruction (Teacher's Manual) 21
    Production of Educational Talking Pictures Used in the
      Experiment 21

III. RESULTS OF FINAL TESTS 23
    Statistical Techniques Employed 23
    Gains in Natural Science 24
    Gains in Music 26
    Specific Contribution of the Talking Picture 28
    Test Items Not Answered in Natural Science Pictures . . 34
    Results of Complete Final Tests 34
    Summary of Results 37

IV. EFFECTIVENESS OF THE TALKING PICTURE IN GROUPS OF
      BELOW AVERAGE AND ABOVE AVERAGE INTELLIGENCE 38
    Test Results of Low and High Intelligence Groups in
      Natural Science 39

CONTENTS

CHAPTER   PAGE

Final Test Gains over Initial Tests in Natural Science .   39
Gains on Picture-Unit Items in Natural Science   39
Gains on Non-Picture Items in Natural Science   39
Relative Superiority of Experimental Over Control
     Groups in Mean Gains in Natural Science   41
Test Results of Low and High Intelligence Groups in Music   41
Final Test Gains Over Initial Tests in Music   41
Gains on Picture-Unit Items in Music   43
Gains on Non-Picture Items in Music   43
Relative Superiority of Experimental Over Control
     Groups in Mean Gains in Music   43
Summary   44

V. RESULTS OF RECALL TESTS   45
Recall Test Gains Over Initial Tests in Natural Science . .   45
Recall Test Gains Over Initial Tests in Music   48
Recall Test Gains on Picture-Unit Items   48
Recall Test Gains on Non-Picture Items   51
Per Cent of Retention from Final Test   53
Summary   54

VI. EFFECTIVENESS OF SPECIFIC ELEMENTS OF PICTURE COM-
     POSITION OF THE FILMS USED IN THE EXPERIMENT .   55
Method of Analyzing Composition Elements   70
Results of Analysis of Comparative Elements   71
     Type of Photography   71
     Focal Length of Scenes   71
     Scene Length   72
     Quality of Lighting   72
     Speech, Other Sound, and Picture   73
     Section of Film in Which Scene Occurred   74
     Repetition   75
     Integration of Audio-Visual Elements   75
Summary   78
Suggestions for Further Research in Sound Film Compo-
     sition   78

VII. SUMMARY   80
Description of Experiment   80
Results of Final Tests   82
Effectiveness of the Talking Pictures in Groups of Below
     Average and Above Average Intelligence Levels   85
Results of Recall Tests   86

CHAPTER   PAGE

Effectiveness of Specific Elements of Talking Picture Composition of the Films Used in the Experiment   87
Summary   88

VIII. PROBLEMS FOR FUTURE RESEARCH   89
Extension of the Range of Present Curriculum   89
Selection of Methods of Subject-Matter Presentation . .   91
Refinement of Testing   92
Other Problems for Research   93

BIBLIOGRAPHY   95

APPENDIX   97
A. Typical Unit of Instruction   99
B. Typical Sound Picture Continuity 108
C. Typical Initial Subject Matter Test 113
D. Tables Showing Complete Data 117

MEASURING THE EFFECTIVENESS OF SOUND PICTURES AS TEACHING AIDS

CHAPTER I

INTRODUCTION

THE recent development of sound pictures suggests many possibilities concerning their use as an aid in classroom instruction. With the introduction of this new medium into the educational field should go a well-planned, comprehensive program of research. This research should include not only the measurement of the value of such an aid but also a careful appraisal of existing pictures for the purpose of improving production techniques and thereby increasing the value of sound pictures as educational tools.

HISTORICAL BACKGROUND

Several studies have already been made which indicate some important contributions of sound pictures to education. The number of such studies is rather limited, however, for sound pictures are an innovation in the educational world. A brief summary and critical evaluation of the more important educational sound picture experimentation will give some idea of how far the work has progressed.

The Middlesex Experiment

The first experiment with educational talking pictures was probably the one conducted in Middlesex County,[1] England, by a committee which included representatives of the Local Education Committee and the National Union of Teachers under the general supervision of the Psychological and Educational Research Committee of the Executive of the Union.

[1] A complete report of this study will be found in *Sound Films in Schools.* "The Schoolmaster" Publishing Co., Fleet Street, London, England, 1931. Pp. 120.

The main objective of this study was to discover the place which sound films might ultimately occupy in schools, assuming that suitable picture material would be forthcoming. This involved some comparison of the educational effectiveness of both sound and silent films. The experimenters investigated the utility of films as a teaching medium as well as a means of arousing interest on the part of the pupils. Particular emphasis was given to the task of ascertaining whether or not sound films open up new channels for the presentation of ideas to the backward child.

Classified according to subjects the films used were: geography, six; natural science, four; and films of general interest dealing with outstanding events and personalities of modern life, six. All films had been produced for adult entertainment, so their usefulness as educational tools was in some respects limited.

Fifteen schools—four primary, nine senior, and two secondary —coöperated in the experiment. More than 3,500 pupils and 180 teachers participated.

All classes, each having fewer than fifty pupils, were shown the films, some once and some twice. The number of presentations was left to each teacher's discretion. Each class was divided into two sections, one receiving a preparatory lesson, the other having no preparatory work before the film was shown. The same test situation was set up for a recapitulatory lesson. Essay examinations were sent to all schools and each teacher scored her own pupils' tests. Pupils were tested not only immediately after the conclusion of the picture study but also after a lapse of a number of days. Questionnaires were sent to all the teachers to obtain their comments on the results of the films as these were revealed in the reactions of the pupils and in their own impressions of the pictures.

The answers to the questionnaires indicated that the teachers were generally agreed that this new medium of instruction stimulated the pupils to greater activity. The teachers were also agreed that this medium aided perceptibly in learning. Most of the teachers preferred the sound film to the silent film for educational purposes. The teachers of backward pupils were particularly enthusiastic in their praise of the sound film.

The test results, however, are subject to criticism. Each

teacher scored his own examinations which, of necessity, resulted in errors due to subjective judgment. No control group was used nor were initial tests given prior to the experiment to determine what or how much information was possessed by the pupils concerning the subjects.

The outstanding contribution of this experiment was apparently the stimulation of the study of the need for educational talking pictures better adapted to classroom needs.

Fox Film Experiment

In July, 1931, the Fox Film Corporation enlisted the coöperation of the United States Office of Education and George Washington University in testing the value of educational talking pictures.[2] One boy and one girl were sent to Washington from each state; in each case they were selected by the governor of the state. Five of the Fox films were used in the experiment: "Toads," 1 reel; "The Monarch Butterfly," 1 reel; "Volcanoes," 3 reels; "Glaciers," 3 reels; "River Valleys," 4 reels. A test of fifty questions (forty true-false and ten multiple-choice) was constructed for each picture.

The experimentation extended over a period of four days. On the first day all the tests were given to the children. On the second day two films were shown and the appropriate two tests repeated. On the third day two more films were shown and the corresponding tests repeated. On the fourth day one film and its test were given.

The average gain per pupil on all five tests was 17.7 points, and since there were fifty questions in each test, the experimenters concluded that this represented a 35 per cent gain due to the effect of the educational sound pictures.

This experiment indicated a definite contribution made by sound pictures when used as a means of classroom instruction. The extent of this contribution is questionable, however, since no control group was used as a basis for comparison. Eighty per cent of the test questions were of the true-false type. These questions were repeated from one to three days after the initial tests were administered, not insuring against the element of test teaching. It should also be noted that the intelligence and social background of the pupils participating in this experiment were

[2] Reported in the pamphlet, *Sound Motion Pictures as a Factor in Education.* Fox Film Corporation, New York City, 1931. Pp. 11.

undoubtedly considerably above the average, because of the manner in which the pupils participating in the experiment were selected.

Experiment by Dr. C. C. Clark

Dr. C. C. Clark[3] of New York University studied the relative effectiveness of sound pictures, silent motion pictures, and classroom lecture demonstrations. Approximately six hundred freshman students attending the 1931 spring session and the 1932 winter session of the science survey courses at the School of Commerce, Accounts and Finance of New York University participated in the experiment.

Thirteen films were used in the investigation, seven in the field of biological science and six in the field of physical science. The biological science films were produced primarily for theatrical purposes and adult entertainment; the physical science films for general use—cultural and educational. None of them was produced to fit into any specific course of study or according to any definite classroom procedure. Their values, then, for experimental purposes in a classroom situation were somewhat limited.

Of the biological science films three originally were silent films converted to sound films by superimposing a popular lecture. The speech and the silent titles were not identical, however, the speech being somewhat more pertinent and complete. Both editions—sound and silent—were available and were used in comparing the effectiveness of sound and silent pictures in a classroom situation. The titles were: "Castles of Paper—Habits and Characteristics of Insects," "Why Eyes Tell Lies—Optical Illusions," and "Killing the Killer—Habits and Characteristics of the Cobra and Mongoose." The other four biological science pictures were: "The Great Apes" and "Life in the Sea," silent pictures, and "Monkeys" and "Beavers," sound pictures. These two silent films and two sound films were also used in comparing the relative effects of sound and silent pictures. It is apparent that the silent pictures used in this phase of the experiment were not completely comparable with the sound pictures.

[3] Clark, C. C., *Sound Motion Pictures as an Aid in Classroom Teaching: A Comparative Study of Their Effectiveness at the Junior College Level of Instruction.* New York University School of Commerce, Accounts and Finance; unpublished Doctor's dissertation.

Six films, three sound and three silent, in the field of physical science were compared with classroom lectures and demonstrations set up by the New York University instructors participating in this experiment in imitation of the films. The sound films used in this phase of the experiment were originally produced as sound films, the sound being an integral part of the film. They were: "Characteristics of Sound," "Liquid Air," and "Radio-active Substances." The three silent films were: "Wizardry of Wireless," "Revelations by X-rays," and "Electro-Magnetism."

The group of students was divided into experimental groups and control groups equated on the basis of an intelligence and a vocabulary test. Each of the four regular class instructors taught both experimental and control groups during the entire experiment. No additional teaching, apart from the film material or the "identical" classroom lectures, took place.

Two types of measuring devices were employed. One consisted of a battery of written tests; the other was a photographic record of the classes made immediately after each of a series of distracting auditory or visual stimuli. A count of the heads turned away from the screen or demonstrator was used as a measure of the students' sustained attention affected by the type of instruction used. The written tests were designed to measure three phases of the problem investigated: concrete knowledge or information, ability to think more accurately and to reason more soundly, and interest in the topic studied.

Following are the conclusions drawn by Clark from the results of his study. The first six conclusions are concerned with that phase of the experiment in which three sound and three silent physical science films were compared with lecture demonstrations set up in imitation of the film material. The last conclusion is concerned with a comparison of the sound and silent biological science pictures.

1. Educational sound films of the type in which the sound is a vital and realistic part of the picture are as effective as identical lecture demonstrations in conveying specific information to mature students.

2. Silent films similar to those used in this investigation appear to be less effective for developing specific knowledge than identical classroom demonstrations.

3. The sound and silent films in the field of physical science are as effective as their corresponding lecture demonstrations in the development of ability to think more clearly and to reason more soundly.

4. In maintaining interests already possessed by the students, as expressed by them on an interest test, these sound films and the silent films appear to be about equally effective but have a slight advantage over the lecture demonstrations.

5. In stimulating new interests, the sound films, silent films, and lecture demonstrations used are about equally effective, with a small advantage indicated in favor of the sound films.

6. A measure of sustained attention on the part of the students indicated that the sound films in the field of the physical sciences are more effective than the silent films and demonstrations used.

7. When sound films of the lecture type are compared with identical silent films, the sound films are less effective than the silent films in conveying specific information.

It will be recalled that the sound and silent films used in the experiment were not completely comparable. The sound versions of the three films "Castles of Paper," "Why Eyes Tell Lies," and "Killing the Killer" were not identical with the silent versions. The limited number of questions measuring these two media of instruction tested only the subject matter common to the two kinds of films. The investigator found the difference in average scores between the two groups to be but 0.5, which difference is not statistically certain as favoring either group.[4]

The comparison made between the two sound pictures "Monkeys" and "Beavers" and the two silent pictures "The Great Apes" and "Life in the Sea" was invalid because the picture material was different for each of the four films and because a different set of test questions was used to measure each group. It was by means of this invalid comparison that the investigator found a statistically certain difference in average test score favoring the group observing the two silent pictures. The difference in test scores may have been due to the fact that the test questions administered to the group observing the two sound pictures may have been more difficult than those administered

---

[4] The experimental constant was 3.5, which does not indicate that there was a statistically certain difference between the two groups.

to the group observing the two silent pictures or that the material in the silent pictures may have been presented in a more vivid and interesting manner. A valid investigation of the comparative effects of sound and silent films would utilize completely comparable sound and silent pictures, their effect being measured by a battery of highly reliable and valid tests.

The outstanding contribution of this experiment was the definite effort to measure reliably areas hitherto untouched.

Erpi Experiment in Teacher Training[5]

During the summer session, 1931, of Teachers College, Columbia University, Dr. Eads and Mr. Stover of the Research Staff of Erpi Picture Consultants, Inc., conducted an experiment with four classes in educational psychology to determine whether educational talking pictures could add to the usual classroom procedure in teacher-training courses. The film used was "Individual Differences in Arithmetic," a twenty-minute talking picture by Dr. Guy T. Buswell of the University of Chicago, in which he describes and demonstrates various techniques for diagnosing difficulties in arithmetic.

In order to obtain a measure of the influence of the talking picture as an aid in learning, this experiment was planned to answer the following four questions:

1. Does a combination of reading assignment and talking picture enable students to gain a clearer understanding of the subject than that obtained from reading only?

2. Does the presentation of a subject by means of specific reading, class discussion of the reading, and observation of a talking picture give better results than those obtained from a combination of reading and discussion only?

3. Does the presentation of a twenty-minute talking picture before students unfamiliar with the subject give better results than those obtained from a twenty-minute lecture personally delivered by an expert in the field?

4. Does the presentation of a twenty-minute talking picture enable students to gain a clearer understanding of a subject than that obtained from reading the material on which the picture was based?

The number of students participating in each of the above

[5] Eads, Laura Krieger and Stover, Edgar M., *Talking Pictures in Teacher Training.* Erpi Picture Consultants, Inc., New York City, unpublished.

phases of the experiment was 99, 21, 50, and 70, respectively. Some of the students in the first experimental group saw the picture twice, some saw it once only; all of the students in the second experimental group saw the picture twice; the students in the third and fourth experimental groups saw the picture once only.

The results of this experiment may be briefly summarized as follows:

1. Seventy-seven per cent of the students who saw the talking picture twice made a score higher than the average score of those who did not see the picture.

2. Seventy-two per cent of the students who saw the picture twice made a score higher than the average score of those who saw the picture only once.

3. Fifty-six per cent of the students who saw the picture once made a score higher than the average score of those who did not see the picture.

4. Eighty per cent of the students who saw the picture, read the monograph on which the picture was based, and took part in class discussion of the monograph made a score higher than the average of those who read the monograph and participated in class discussion, but did not see the picture.

5. Sixty-eight per cent of the students who saw the twenty-minute talking picture only made a score higher than the average of those who listened to only a twenty-minute lecture based on the monograph.

6. Sixty per cent of the students who saw the twenty-minute talking picture but did not read the monograph, made a score higher than the average of those who spent on the average 2.61 hours reading the monograph.

This experiment was the first of a series to test the merits of the talking picture as a teaching medium. In addition to revealing the efficacy of this particular film as an aid in teacher training, the results of the experiment threw some light on the relative merits of various measuring devices which are applicable in investigations of this nature.

Despite the fact that this preliminary experiment was limited, owing to the small number of students participating, these results seem to indicate a definite contribution of the educational talking picture in teacher-training work.

THE PROBLEM OF THIS STUDY

The purpose of the present study is twofold and may be summarized thus:

1. To determine by experimentation the relative effectiveness (a) of teaching with the aid of certain educational talking pictures in the fields of natural science and music in grades 5 and 7, respectively, and (b) of the usual methods of classroom instruction.

2. To make an analysis of the composition elements of certain scenes of the talking pictures used in the experiment, this analysis being treated in such a manner as to serve as an introduction to the study of the relative effectiveness of these elements of composition.

CHAPTER II

DESCRIPTION OF EXPERIMENT

As THE previous discussion shows, there is need for further evidence regarding the value of sound films produced for teaching purposes and used in actual teaching situations. Another factor which is highly important in the future development of sound films is a careful appraisal of the composition elements inherent in such films. This study will suggest, therefore, the possible lines of procedure along which such an investigation may be pursued.

SCOPE OF THE STUDY

The present study is limited to the subject matter fields of natural science and music. The natural science sound films used were produced primarily for the elementary school level while the music sound films were produced primarily for the junior high school level. Classes in the second half-year of the fifth grade participated in the experiment using the natural science films, and classes in the second half-year of the seventh grade participated in experiment using music films. Each subject matter field was limited to four topics, or units of instruction. The natural science units were: Butterflies, Beetles, Amphibians, and Growth of Plants. The music units were those comprising the symphony orchestra series: the String Choir, the Woodwind Choir, the Brass Choir, and the Percussion Group.

Approximately 950 fifth grade pupils in 32 classes, 1,425 seventh grade pupils in the same number of classes, and 64 teachers participated in the experiment.

THE TECHNIQUE FOLLOWED

The experimental-control technique utilizing the equated-teacher method was followed throughout the experiment. The pupils in the control groups were taught by the ordinary classroom methods without the aid of educational talking pictures.

The pupils in the experimental groups were presented with three showings of each picture during the regular class periods. This type of procedure was intended to eliminate any transfer of teaching method suggested by the films themselves from experimental to control groups through the teachers. This procedure, however, did require the selection of a sufficient number of classroom teachers to eliminate differences in ability which may have escaped the local school authorities, who attempted to match experimental classes with those control classes having teachers whom they considered to be equal in ability to the teachers of the experimental group. A further check on the ability of the teachers participating in the experiment will be discussed later in this chapter.

THE EDUCATIONAL SOUND PICTURES USED

The content of the films used in this experiment included those important elements of subject matter selected from basic units of instruction[1] which, it was felt, were particularly well adapted to presentation through the medium of the sound film, all available teaching devices and production techniques inherent in sound film production being considered. Other criteria which guided the selection and manner of presentation of specific elements of subject matter in these pictures were suggested by the "Standards for Educational Talking Pictures and Supplementary Materials."[2]

TYPES OF SUBJECT MATTER TESTS

Tests were constructed from the units of instruction. Those elements of subject matter which were considered important by science and music specialists who prepared the units of instruction were submitted as the basis for the tests. Using these items of subject matter, tests of the following types were constructed for each unit studied.[3]

1. *Graphic representation.* These tests were designed to measure the pupil's ability to recognize various phases of animal and

---

[1] These Units of Instruction were prepared and published by the Research Staff of Erpi Picture Consultants, Inc., 250 West 57th Street, New York City, and are available at this address.

[2] Standards prepared and published by the Research Staff of Erpi Picture Consultants, Inc., and available at the above address.

[3] Samples of the test items are included in Chapter VI. One complete initial subject matter test is reproduced in Appendix C.

plant life and the more concrete elements of the instruments of the symphony orchestra.

2. *Essay completion.* This type of test required one or more phrases or sentences in order to furnish a complete answer.

3. *One-word completion.* These tests required the insertion of one word to complete statements regarding the items of subject matter.

4. *Multiple choice.* This type of test required the checking of one of four responses which correctly completed a given statement.

5. *Two choice.* This type of test was the same form as the multiple choice except that there were two responses instead of four from which to choose.

6. *True-false.* This type of test was used to measure concepts which could not be measured easily by one of the other five types of tests.

The weighting assigned to the various types of test items is given below:[4]

TYPE OF ITEMS	WEIGHT
True-false	1
Two choice	1
Multiple choice	2
One-word completion	3
Essay completion	5
Graphic representation (weighting varied according to the type of above tests which the item most nearly represented)	

PRELIMINARY TESTING

Eight tests were constructed from the units, each consisting of approximately 150 items of the types previously described. The tests in natural science were administered as preliminary tests to more than 350 pupils in the second half of the fifth grade; the music tests to more than 250 pupils in the second half of the seventh grade. All tests were administered in cities and villages within the metropolitan area.* The purpose of this

[4] A group of eleven advanced research students in test construction under the direction of Professor Rudolf Pintner, Teachers College, Columbia University, conferred with the writer to determine the weighting of test items. The weightings assigned were arrived at statistically rather than according to the relative importance of the subject matter measured. It was felt that a statistical weighting was less subject to errors of subjective judgment.

* Certain schools within the following cities participated in the preliminary testing: New York City, Pelham, N. Y., New Rochelle, N. Y., White Plains, N. Y., Peekskill, N. Y., and Pleasantville, N. Y.

preliminary testing was to devise initial tests to be given prior to the experimental instruction. After scoring, the items were arranged in order of difficulty. Those which were ambiguous and those which were found to be either too simple or too complex for the specific grade levels were omitted. The preliminary testing also allowed the computation of rough indications of the reliability of the initial tests. From the preliminary tests, scoring keys also were constructed. Each of the resultant initial tests contained approximately fifty items.

The preliminary tests were repeated after the pupils had studied each unit. The results of this testing served as a basis for the construction of each of the final tests to be given after the study of each unit. The final tests consisted of approximately one hundred items each. The number of items in the final tests was greater than that in the initial tests for two reasons: first, to minimize as much as possible the teaching effect of the initial tests, and, second, to measure a broader scope of subject matter than was practical at the time the initial tests were administered.

Recall tests were administered fourteen weeks after the initial tests. This series of tests was identical with the initial tests.

SCORING THE TESTS

All tests, initial, final, and recall, were scored by individuals whose educational experience enabled them to perform this task with a minimum of error. The accuracy of scoring was further insured by one scorer checking another. All scoring was done by means of objective keys which were constructed before the beginning of the experiment on the basis of responses made by the groups of pupils participating in the preliminary testing. It was possible to score objectively, and yet give partial credit to some responses made by pupils in the case of one-word completion and essay completion tests.

RELIABILITY OF THE TESTS

Coefficients of reliability[5] were computed for all the initial, final, and recall tests. In this computation, a random selection

[5] The coefficients of reliability were computed by correlating the odd items with the even items and applying the Spearman-Brown prophecy formula. $\left(r_x = \dfrac{n_r}{1 + (n-1)_r} \right)$

of one hundred test papers was made for each unit. The co-efficients of reliability follow.

UNIT OF INSTRUCTION	INITIAL TEST	FINAL TEST	RECALL TEST
Butterflies	.59	.90	.83
Beetles	.56	.91	.80
Amphibians	.76	.73	.80
Growth of Plants	.64	.90	.84
String Choir	.70	.88	.76
Woodwind Choir	.89	.82	.83
Brass Choir	.68	.89	.87
Percussion Group	.82	.94	.82
Total Science Tests	.84	.98	.88
Total Music Tests	.91	.96	.95

SELECTION OF CITIES PARTICIPATING IN THE EXPERIMENT

Large cities were chosen for the experiment because they offered opportunities (1) to obtain a heterogeneous population, (2) to match teachers more accurately on the basis of teaching ability, and (3) to match classes on the basis of their ability and socio-economic status. In addition, it was necessary to select cities in which were offered junior high school music programs. Cities from three states were chosen in order to compensate for any marked variation in the state courses of study. The cities selected were New York City; Schenectady, N. Y.; Camden, N. J.; Elizabeth, N. J.; and Baltimore, Md. A selected number of fifth and seventh grade classes from each city participated in the experiment. (Hereafter these cities will be designated by the capital letters A, B, C, D, E, but *not* in the order given above.)

SELECTION OF INDIVIDUAL CLASSES AND TEACHERS

The selection of classes by the local authorities was made on the following basis. Classes matched according to intelligence were used in pairs, one class the control, the other the experimental. In the selection of classes consideration was given also to the social background of the pupils. For instance, experimental classes from industrial sections of the city were matched with control classes from similar sections. Experimental classes from residential centers were matched with control classes from similar centers.

Teachers who, in the judgment of local authorities, were comparable in ability, preferably average, were selected for experimental and control groups. Although it was recognized that this selection would not produce a scientifically exact equation of teachers, it was felt that the large number of teachers would tend to minimize the effect of variations in ability of individual teachers. A total of sixty-four classroom teachers participated in the experiment.[6] To supplement the purely subjective judgments of the local school officers who selected the teachers, the Jacobs[7] rating scale of teaching ability was employed. This scale was used by supervisors and principals to determine more objectively the relative ability of the various teachers chosen. With the exception of one city, the average of the two ratings was computed for each teacher. In this city teachers were rated by their principals only, since a ruling of the local board of education forbade supervisory staff members to provide ratings for use outside the school system.

There are five major divisions on the Jacobs scale having a numerical value of from one to ten points for each of the categories of traits considered desirable in effective teaching. The value assigned to each of these categories by the rater is multiplied by a coefficient in order to obtain a weighting of that category. The sum of the weighted values represents the rating assigned to the teacher. Table I shows that in this experiment the difference between the two groups of teachers (control and experimental) was negligible. For both the natural science and music teachers, the composite average for the five cities was slightly in favor of the control teachers, two-tenths of one point of a possible total of 100 points for the natural science teachers and three points for the music teachers.

RESULTS OF INTELLIGENCE TEST

The mental ability of the pupils participating in the experiment was measured by the Pintner Rapid Survey Test, Form B. The average class results for this test corresponded very closely

---

[6] Four of the sixty-four classes, two experimental and one control class in music and one control class in natural science, were omitted from the total test results because they did not adhere to experimental conditions.

[7] Jacobs, C. L. *The Relation of the Teacher's Education to Her Effectiveness*, p. 39. Bureau of Publications, Teachers College, Columbia University, New York City, 1928. Pp. 97.

TABLE I

MEAN SCORES OF TEACHERS OF NATURAL SCIENCE AND MUSIC
CLASSES ON BASIS OF JACOBS' RATING SCALE

| SUBJECT | CITIES | | | | | | | | | | COMBINED CITIES | |
| | A | | B | | C | | D† | | E | | | |
	Exp.	Cont.	Exp.	Cont.	Exp.	Cont.	Exp.	Cont.	Exp.	Cont.	Exp.	Cont.
Natural Science												
No. of teachers .	4	3*	3	3	3	3	3	3	3	3	16	15
Mean	76.8	68.9	71.3	62.9	79.5	85.2	66.3	73.3	70.8	76.6	73.2	73.4
Music												
No. of teachers .	3	3	1	1	2	2	4	3	5	5	15	14
Mean	69.8	75.9	72.0	56.0	70.6	61.7	76.5	75.2	63.3	75.3	69.8	72.8

* Teacher omitted rated 61.1. See footnote 6, page 15.
† Not all ratings available for music teachers in City D.

with those intelligence quotients available in the records of the local schools. It was not practical to compute the average scores on intelligence tests administered previously and the Pintner Test results because in more than one-third of the classes no intelligence scores were available. Table II gives the results of the intelligence testing.

As indicated in Table II, there was a slight difference in the mean intelligence quotients favoring the experimental group in the case of the natural science classes for the combined cities.[8] This difference can not, however, be considered statistically significant (critical ratio of the difference between the means, 1.88). In music, there was a statistically significant difference favoring the combined control groups (critical ratio, 3.06).[9]

RESULTS OF INITIAL TESTS[10]

As previously stated, the initial tests for the eight units were administered by a member of the local school staff trained in this procedure. They were given to all control and experimental classes in the five cities. In no case were the classroom teachers allowed to administer or to see the actual test materials. The

[8] In a check as to whether this slight difference would affect final results a sufficient number of cases were omitted to result in equal mean intelligence quotients for both experimental and control group. These data are given in the Appendix. Total natural science test data are given in Table E of the Appendix.

[9] A critical ratio of 3.00 or more indicates practical certainty that a true difference exists in the same direction.

[10] A copy of one of the initial subject matter tests *Amphibians* is reproduced in Appendix C.

TABLE II

PINTNER INTELLIGENCE TEST SCORES FOR EXPERIMENTAL AND CONTROL GROUPS IN NATURAL SCIENCE AND MUSIC

SUBJECT	CITIES										COMBINED CITIES	
	A		B		C		D		E			
	Exp.	Cont.	Exp.	Cont.	Exp.	Cont.	Exp.	Cont.	Exp.	Cont.	Exp.	Cont.
Natural Science												
No. of cases	93	66	68	82	63	79	60	70	81	70	365	367
Mean	105.46	103.10	101.22	102.26	104.30	105.58	103.38	94.22	112.78	111.86	105.78	103.54
Critical ratio	.82*			.46		.46	3.54		.45		1.88	
Music												
No. of cases	71	77	26	17	85	94	98	93	230	344	510	625
Mean	98.96	101.44	100.26	101.02	101.36	102.82	94.66	98.20	100.82	102.64	99.42	101.84
Critical ratio		1.32		.19		.70		2.16		1.54		3.06

* In this and similar tables the critical ratio is entered in the column having the higher mean.

TABLE III

INITIAL TEST SCORES MADE BY EXPERIMENTAL AND CONTROL GROUPS

NATURAL SCIENCE

UNIT	CITIES										COMBINED CITIES	
	A		B		C		D		E			
	Exp.	Cont.	Exp.	Cont.	Exp.	Cont.	Exp.	Cont.	Exp.	Cont.	Exp.	Cont.
Butterflies												
No. of cases	104	78	92	104	76	95	87	82	104	93	463	452
Mean	21.14	21.40	21.34	22.32	22.86	24.94	19.36	18.58	23.12	23.96	21.58	22.36
Critical ratio		.25		1.18		1.98	.90			.92		1.81
Beetles												
No. of cases	100	77	82	101	70	98	85	87	96	97	433	460
Mean	16.99	19.39	17.32	18.02	17.59	18.24	15.01	13.70	21.43	19.39	17.55	17.43
Critical ratio		.46		.84		.77	.52		1.94		.30	
Amphibians												
No. of cases	104	76	84	97	76	95	72	81	102	105	438	454
Mean	28.80	29.38	31.86	33.06	30.48	33.48	23.98	22.76	37.02	36.72	30.62	31.86
Critical ratio		.36		.85		1.78	1.03		.19			1.65
Growth of Plants												
No. of cases	107	77	92	104	77	100	88	85	100	108	464	474
Mean	23.04	24.18	28.96	29.38	27.14	34.70	27.50	26.00	32.46	35.40	27.76	30.42
Critical ratio		.94		.30		5.32	.88			1.87		3.75
Total Science												
No. of cases	93	66	68	82	63	79	60	70	81	70	365	367
Mean	90.35	87.25	100.15	102.15	98.50	108.90	85.35	80.80	115.45	115.35	98.35	100.65
Critical ratio	.76			.52		2.42	1.11		.02			1.13

results of the initial testing are given in Tables III and IV. These results indicate that there was a difference in scores favoring the control groups in both the natural science and music initial tests. This difference was greater in the case of the music tests.

TEACHING PROCEDURE AND TIME ALLOTMENTS

Instructions regarding teaching procedure and time allotments were given to the local supervisors of the experiment in all cities. These instructions were intended to furnish the basis for uniformity in teaching and supervision throughout the experiment.

Teachers of the control groups were free to use any instructional device available with the exception of motion pictures. (Experimental teachers agreed to meet, view, and make notes on all sound pictures used, at least one week before beginning their instruction on the subject of the picture.) Teachers of neither experimental nor control groups were allowed to learn about the nature of any of the tests until the experiment was concluded.

The school principals coöperated in supervising the administration of all tests used. All teachers and principals were provided with copies of the units of instruction and schedules pertaining to their particular subjects and groups. Schedules were made as complete as possible to provide for uniform periods of time elapsing between teaching periods.

The class teaching of each of the four units in both natural science and music began two weeks after the administration of the intelligence and initial tests. Each unit was taught within a two weeks' period.

Each science unit extended over a period of 150 minutes of instruction, divided into five thirty-minute periods for both experimental and control groups. At the end of each unit a final test was given covering the unit. The experimental groups had three ten-minute picture showings, scheduled for the first, third, and fifth periods of each unit. Thus their actual teaching time was reduced to 120 minutes. The showings were preceded or followed by discussion of the picture aims and content.

The time allotted each music unit was also 150 minutes of instruction, divided into three forty-five minute periods, with a concluding fifteen-minute instructional period. The experimental groups had a ten-minute picture showing during each of the

TABLE IV

INITIAL TEST SCORES MADE BY EXPERIMENTAL AND CONTROL GROUPS

MUSIC

UNIT	A Exp.	A Cont.	B Exp.	B Cont.	C Exp.	C Cont.	D Exp.	D Cont.	E* Exp.	E* Cont.	Cities A to D Combined Exp.	Cities A to D Combined Cont.
String Choir												
No. of cases	93	92	33	23	100	121	126	123	110	147	462	506
Mean	48.44	47.16	31.12	40.02	41.68	42.30	27.70	31.90	39.06	42.42	37.90	40.58
Critical ratio	.72			2.76		.37		3.23		2.55		3.23
Woodwinds												
No. of cases	90	93	30	23	102	110	137	127	107	148	466	501
Mean	37.34	32.76	24.70	25.24	29.82	36.00	14.24	18.64	24.02	29.76	25.38	27.16
Critical ratio	2.62			.19		3.32		4.11		3.90		2.02
Brasses												
No. of cases	89	83	29	23	101	123	175	120	199	228	593	577
Mean	35.94	30.76	33.44	34.20	33.24	33.46	22.36	23.86	22.72	28.08	26.92	28.98
Critical ratio	3.18			.32		.14		1.29		5.10		2.99
Percussion												
No. of cases	89	97	31	21	99	120	160	120	148	214	527	572
Mean	37.18	36.88	38.20	42.26	34.76	41.24	27.62	32.64	27.26	30.34	31.10	34.66
Critical ratio	.14			1.13		3.68		3.12		2.23		4.29
Total Music												
No. of cases	71	77	26	17	85	94	98	93	Cities	A to D	280	281
Mean	156.14	147.86	125.12	136.58	140.78	152.84	89.54	108.86			125.30	135.92
Critical ratio	1.37			1.19		2.02		3.98				2.90

* In City E only two of the music units were taught experimentally to each class, owing to the fact that local class schedules would not permit a more complete participation in this section of the study. Four of these classes studied the units String Choir and Woodwind Choir; the other six classes studied the units Brass Choir and Percussion Group.

first, second, and last periods, reducing their teaching time to 120 minutes.

THE UNIT OF INSTRUCTION (TEACHER'S MANUAL)[11]

All teachers, both experimental and control, were furnished with identical units of instruction which were to serve as guides in the teaching of all units. These teachers' manuals were developed as part of the project of preparing and producing the talking pictures used in the experiment. Before the production of any picture was begun, a unit of instruction was prepared. It was intended to provide the teacher with a guide for the teaching of the unit, a guide which was easy to use and which offered numerous suggestions for the enrichment of pupil learning. The outline for a typical unit of instruction is given below:

    I. Objectives
       A. Generalizations to be developed
       B. Specific objectives
   II. Suggested Approaches
 III. Essential Meanings, Information, and Materials to Be Used in Developing the Theme
       A. Overview, giving necessary background for the unit
       B. Outline summary of content
       C. Development of content
  IV. Suggested Learning Situations or Pupil Experiences Through Which the Generalizations May Be Developed
   V. Possible Problems to Be Used in Gathering Data
  VI. Suggestions for Evaluating Teaching Units
 VII. General Bibliography for Teachers and Pupils

PRODUCTION OF EDUCATIONAL TALKING PICTURES USED IN THE EXPERIMENT

Following the preparation of a unit of instruction, a critical analysis was made of the unit to determine those elements of subject matter which lent themselves particularly well to effective presentation through the medium of the talking picture. From this analysis, the materials of the film were selected and developed into a suitable continuity[12] which served as the basis

[11] The standards which serve to guide in the preparation of the units of instruction were prepared and published by the Research Staff of Erpi Picture Consultants, Inc. These are available at the office of this organization at 250 West 57th St., New York City. The unit of instruction *Amphibians* is reproduced in Appendix A.

[12] The continuity for the sound film *Percussion Group* furnished in Appendix B illustrates the type of films used in the experiment.

for the final production of the talking picture subjects. The standards controlling the preparation and production of the educational talking picture, as well as a check list for the evaluation of the completed film, were prepared and published by the Research Staff of Erpi Picture Consultants, Inc.

CHAPTER III

RESULTS OF FINAL TESTS

IN THIS experiment great care was exercised to construct valid tests[1] of high reliability. It will be recalled that the final tests contained more items than the initial tests. Approximately 65 per cent of the items of the four initial tests in natural science were reproduced in the final tests. The remaining items of the initial tests in natural science were matched in the final tests with other items on the basis of the percentage of pupils answering the items correctly on the preliminary test. Consequently, a large proportion of the final tests in natural science was equivalent to the total initial tests. This section of the complete final tests in natural science will hereafter be designated as Final Test I, as distinguished from the Complete Final Test. All the items of the initial tests in music were reproduced in the final music tests. This section of the complete final tests in music will hereafter also be designated as Final Test I. The differences between the scores made by the pupils on the Initial Test and on Final Test I for each unit indicate the amount of measurable information *gained* by those pupils after a specified number and type of classroom activities had been pursued.

In order to determine whether the educational talking picture when used as an integral part of classroom instruction contributes to learning, a comparison was made between the test results of the experimental and control groups. In the experimental groups part of the allotted instructional periods—one-fifth— was devoted to the presentation of the talking picture. The control groups were, of course, not permitted to see the talking picture during the experiment.

STATISTICAL TECHNIQUES EMPLOYED

The following statistical techniques were employed in treating the data.

[1] See page 11.

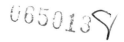

The means, or averages, of the experimental groups' scores were compared with the means of the control groups' scores.

The reliability of the means was determined by computing the standard deviations of the means. Differences between means may not be statistically significant or may be due to chance. In order to determine whether these differences are statistically significant, the critical ratio of the difference between the means of the experimental and control groups was computed (the difference between the means divided by the standard deviation of the difference between the means). A critical ratio of three (3.00) or more indicates practical certainty that a true difference in the same direction exists.

The superiority of one group over the other was computed by dividing the difference between the means of the two groups by the means of the inferior group, and expressing this relation in terms of per cent (per cent superiority).

GAINS IN NATURAL SCIENCE

Table V shows the comparative gains of the experimental and control groups in the natural science units, on the basis of the results on Final Test I and the initial test.

For every unit in every city, with the exception of the unit Growth of Plants in City B, the mean gain of the experimental group is greater than that of the control group. For each unit, considering the combined groups in all cities, the differences in mean gains favoring the experimental groups are statistically significant. The critical ratios range from 5.76[2] in the case of Growth of Plants to 10.77 in the case of Amphibians. The per cents of superiority of experimental over control groups in all cities combined are as follows: Amphibians, 29.7; Growth of Plants, 21.8; Butterflies, 21.7; and Beetles, 20.2.

The results of the Final Test I in all four units combined indicate that in all cities the mean differences in gains favored the experimental groups. The greatest differences between the mean gains of the experimental and control groups existed in City D. This difference may be partly explained by the fact that there was a difference of intelligence in favor of the experimental group. The lowest differences between the gains of the

---

[2] As stated previously, a critical ratio of 3.00, or greater, is sufficiently high to establish the fact that a true difference exists.

TABLE V*

FINAL TEST I GAINS OVER THE INITIAL TEST MADE BY EXPERIMENTAL AND CONTROL GROUPS

NATURAL SCIENCE

| UNIT | CITIES | | | | | | | | | | COMBINED CITIES | |
| | A | | B | | C | | D | | E | | | |
	Exp.	Cont.	Exp.	Cont.	Exp.	Cont.	Exp.	Cont.	Exp.	Cont.	Exp.	Cont.
Butterflies												
No. of cases	104	78	92	104	76	95	87	82	104	93	463	452
Mean gain	43.50	34.41	53.91	51.63	48.63	44.22	53.79	33.21	57.03	41.13	51.39	42.21
Critical ratio	4.71		1.04		1.74		10.61		7.36		8.66	
% superiority	26.4		4.4		10.0		62.0		38.7		21.7	
Beetles												
No. of cases	100	77	82	101	70	98	85	87	96	97	433	460
Mean gain	40.56	29.65	49.76	46.50	40.50	36.72	41.94	24.60	47.13	42.42	44.01	36.60
Critical ratio	4.45		1.55		1.47		7.41		2.37		6.86	
% superiority	36.8		7.0		10.3		70.5		11.1		20.2	
Amphibians												
No. of cases	104	76	84	97	76	95	72	81	102	105	438	454
Mean gain	39.21	30.63	41.25	35.94	33.78	32.67	52.62	30.54	44.25	32.58	42.30	32.61
Critical ratio	4.17		2.58		.56		13.14		6.86		10.77	
% superiority	28.0		14.8		3.4		72.3		35.8		29.7	
Growth of Plants												
No. of cases	107	77	92	104	77	100	88	85	100	108	464	474
Mean gain	33.01	29.82	39.96	46.08	41.19	37.47	43.71	19.59	45.12	31.37	40.83	33.51
Critical ratio	1.02			2.25	1.31		9.73		6.30		5.76	
% superiority	10.7			15.3	9.9		123.1		43.8		21.8	
Total Science												
No. of cases	93	66	68	82	63	79	60	70	81	70	365	367
Mean gain	157.62	124.10	193.46	177.38	168.82	146.34	194.90	108.58	191.86	150.66	179.94	142.90
Critical ratio	3.93		1.96		2.44		12.40		6.34		9.55	
% superiority	27.0		9.1		15.4		79.5		27.3		25.9	

* Complete tables in Appendix A furnish medians, interquartile range (Q), standard deviation of the distributions, standard deviation of the means, and differences between means, in addition to the information furnished in this table.

two groups existed in City B. It may be noted that for the total tests in natural science in all cities combined, the difference in gains is approximately 37 points, indicating a superiority of experimental over control groups of approximately 26 per cent. The critical ratio of this difference is 9.55.

GAINS IN MUSIC

Table VI shows the comparative gains of the experimental and control groups in the music units. In the case of City E class schedules would permit participation in only two of the units for all pupils. In other words, one half the classes participating in the experiment studied String Choir and Woodwind Choir, and the other half studied Brass Choir and Percussion Group. Because of this situation (although the results of the completed unit tests individually are given for the combined cities), the data for the total music tests, covering all four units, can be given only for Cities A, B, C, and D. This fact must be borne in mind in reading all tables which show results in the music units.

As Table VI indicates, the differences in mean gains of every city in every unit were greater for the experimental groups than for the control groups with the exception of String Choir in City A. This difference in City A is not statistically significant, the critical ratio in this case being 1.71. This case presents an unusual situation in that the results from all the cities indicate that the differences in gains recorded for String Choir ranked second among the gains for all the four units. This is true even though the differences favoring the control group in City A were subtracted from the total mean gains.

An examination of the difference in mean gains of experimental and control groups in City A indicates that after String Choir, there was with each successive unit an increasing difference favoring the experimental groups. For the first unit, String Choir, the difference in mean gains is 3 points in favor of the control groups. For the second unit, this difference slightly favors the experimental group. The differences for Brass Choir and Percussion Group are 5 and 10 points, respectively, in favor of the experimental group.

A possible explanation of this unusual outcome is that the teachers of the control groups in City A may have been unduly

TABLE VI

FINAL TEST I GAINS OVER THE INITIAL TEST MADE BY EXPERIMENTAL AND CONTROL GROUPS

MUSIC

UNIT	A Exp.	A Cont.	B Exp.	B Cont.	C Exp.	C Cont.	D Exp.	D Cont.	E* Exp.	E* Cont.	Combined Exp.	Combined Cont.
String Choir												
No. of cases	93	92	33	23	100	121	126	123	110	147	462	506
Mean gain	20.32	23.52	48.38	24.58	31.30	24.12	34.04	30.02	32.20	18.18	31.28	23.72
Critical ratio		1.71	8.78		4.63		3.24		10.70		9.00	
% superiority		15.7	96.8		38.0		11.2		69.9		31.9	
Woodwind Choir												
No. of cases	90	93	30	23	102	110	137	127	107	148	466	501
Mean gain	26.22	25.74	52.50	34.16	41.40	30.02	43.94	39.28	36.85	27.68	38.86	31.08
Critical ratio	.29		5.23		6.58		2.52		4.90		7.94	
% superiority	1.9		53.7		37.9		11.9		33.1		25.0	
Brass Choir												
No. of cases	89	83	29	23	101	123	175	120	199	288	593	577
Mean gain	33.10	28.30	58.02	30.84	39.86	31.12	40.78	37.94	29.98	28.84	36.70	31.22
Critical ratio	2.26		10.14		4.53		1.63		.73		5.89	
% superiority	17.0		88.1		28.1		7.5		4.0		17.6	
Percussion Group												
No. of cases	89	97	31	21	99	120	160	120	148	214	527	572
Mean gain	47.56	37.16	79.72	44.88	59.00	47.80	55.94	40	43.64	34.62	53.60	40.06
Critical ratio	4.26		9.65		4.85		7.81		4.58		12.31	
% superiority	28.0		77.6		23.4		39.9		26.1		33.8	
Total Music											Cities A to D	
No. of cases	71	77	26	17	85	94	98	93			280	281
Mean gain	128.30	115.94	237.26	133.04	172.64	132.68	174.62	141.80			167.48	131.96
Critical ratio	2.16		12.53		7.43		1.41				9.52	
% superiority	10.7		78.3		30.1		23.1				26.9	

* City E could not be included in combined music test results since the pupils of this city participated in only two units.

stimulated by the feeling of competition aroused at the outset by the experimental situation. This resultant initial zeal of the control teachers seemed gradually to wane during the successive weeks of teaching. The interest of experimental teachers, however, seemed to increase during the successive units.

Considering the results of the combined cities, the differences in mean gains for each unit taught were greater for the experimental groups than for the control groups. These differences in mean gains are all statistically significant. The critical ratios range from 5.89 in the case of the unit, Brass Choir, to 12.31 in the case of the unit, Percussion Group. The per cents of superiority of experimental over control groups in all cities combined, in the case of each unit, are as follows: Percussions, 33.8; Strings, 31.9; Woodwinds, 25.0; Brasses, 17.6.

As indicated by the results of the total tests in all four units for Cities A, B, C, and D (as explained above, the total test results were not available for City E), the differences in mean gains favored the experimental groups. The greatest differences between the mean gains of the experimental and control groups existed in City B. The differences in the intelligence of experimental and control groups in this city, although slight, favored the control groups, so that the intelligence factor does not afford even a partial explanation of the unusual amount of this difference. The lowest differences between the gains of the two groups existed in City A.

It may be noted that for the total music tests in Cities A, B, C, and D combined, the difference in mean gains is 36 points, or a superiority of experimental over control groups of 27 per cent. The critical ratio of this difference is 9.52. These results are approximately the same for the natural science units.

From Table VI it may be seen also that the mean gains made over the initial test in City E favored the experimental groups in every case although this difference is not statistically significant in the case of Brass Choir.

SPECIFIC CONTRIBUTION OF THE TALKING PICTURE

Another outstanding question that suggests itself is: What specific contribution to learning is made by the talking picture alone? One means by which this may be partially determined is the method of comparing the mean gains made by experimental and control groups on those test items the answers to which were furnished directly or indirectly by the talking picture as well as by the units of instruction. An analysis of the tests showed that 60 per cent of the natural science tests and 69 per cent of the music tests were items of this type. Hereafter these test items will be designated "picture-unit items."

Table VII shows the comparative gains in the experimental and control groups in all cities on the picture-unit items in the natural science tests. It will be noted that the differences in mean gains were greater for the experimental group than for the control group in the case of every unit in every city studied.

The data on the several units, considering the scores in combined cities, indicate that the greatest percentage of superiority in gains favoring experimental over control groups existed in the case of Growth of Plants. This seems to indicate that, although the actual gains in scores for the experimental groups were lower in Growth of Plants than in any other unit, the picture in this unit probably contributed more to the development of highly complex concepts, inherent in the study of the unit, than did any other picture. An analysis of the content of this picture reveals that such processes (the identification and significance of which were indicated by accompanying speech) as the actual flowing movements of protoplasm, the growing movements of plant roots, stems, and leaves, the germination of seeds, the fertilization of the ovum, the opening of the flower, the movements of pollen tubes, the phenomenon of osmosis, and the actual contortions of the plant in dying after having been deprived of one of the elements of life, are all presented in such a manner as to clarify the concepts involved. In many cases these ideas are very difficult to present through any other medium at the disposal of the classroom teacher, because of certain human limitations to learning which this picture seems to transcend.

The superiority of the experimental groups in the case of this unit, however, exceeded Butterflies by only 5 per cent and Beetles by 9 per cent.

The superiority of the experimental groups in the case of Amphibians was approximately 41 per cent.

These differences in mean gains favoring the experimental groups of the combined cities are all statistically significant. The critical ratios range from 9.11 to 18.13.

TABLE VII

GAINS MADE BY EXPERIMENTAL AND CONTROL GROUPS ON PICTURE-UNIT ITEMS

NATURAL SCIENCE TESTS

UNIT	CITIES										COMBINED CITIES	
	A		B		C		D		E			
	Exp.	Cont.	Exp.	Cont.	Exp.	Cont.	Exp.	Cont.	Exp.	Cont.	Exp.	Cont.
Butterflies												
No. of cases	104	78	92	104	76	95	87	82	104	93	463	452
Mean gain	26.94	17.92	35.08	23.98	29.92	20.56	32.70	15.32	33.44	22.62	31.60	20.36
Critical ratio	6.63		8.47		6.32		13.58		9.02		18.13	
% superiority	50.3		46.3		45.5		113.4		47.8		55.2	
Beetles												
No. of cases	100	77	82	101	70	98	85	87	96	97	433	460
Mean gain	23.48	12.00	26.54	21.36	21.84	16.10	23.32	9.22	24.50	18.82	23.98	15.84
Critical ratio	8.70		3.87		3.54		10.00		4.34		12.33	
% superiority	95.7		24.3		35.7		152.9		30.2		51.4	
Amphibians												
No. of cases	104	76	84	97	76	95	72	81	102	105	438	454
Mean gain	29.45	21.14	31.04	24.65	26.00	21.53	39.47	22.85	32.06	21.86	31.61	22.46
Critical ratio	4.89		3.94		2.73		11.38		7.91		12.20	
% superiority	39.3		25.9		20.8		72.7		46.7		40.7	
Growth of Plants												
No. of cases	107	77	92	104	77	100	88	85	100	108	464	474
Mean gain	20.00	15.68	21.92	18.80	19.19	13.13	22.73	6.65	20.45	9.44	20.42	12.77
Critical ratio	2.26		1.78		3.48		9.51		6.97		9.11	
% superiority	27.6		16.6		46.2		241.8		116.6		59.9	
Total Science												
No. of cases	93	66	68	82	63	79	60	70	81	70	365	367
Mean gain	99.26	66.14	118.22	87.42	96.22	69.66	117.74	55.58	111.18	73.18	107.90	71.02
Critical ratio	6.28		6.21		4.94		15.05		9.20		16.32	
% superiority	50.1		35.2		38.1		111.8		51.9		51.9	

The differences in mean gains on the picture-unit items of the total natural science tests were greater for the experimental groups than for the control groups for every city. The superiority of the experimental groups was greatest in City D and least in City C. The percentage of superiority of the experimental groups was also greatest in City D—112 per cent—but least in City B—approximately 35 per cent.

The difference in mean gains in all cities combined for the total natural science picture-unit items was approximately 37 points greater for the experimental groups than for the control groups. The superiority of the experimental groups over the control in all cities combined was 52 per cent. The critical ratio is 16.32.

Table VIII presents the gains made by the experimental and control groups in all cities on the picture-unit items in the music tests, that is, items the answers to which, although included in the units of instruction, were also included in the music pictures. The difference in mean gains was greater for the experimental groups than for the control groups in every city for every unit with the exception of String Choir in City A. This exception existed also in the case of the gains over the entire initial tests in music, as was discussed in connection with Table VI. This difference in favor of the control group, however, is not statistically significant, the critical ratio being only 1.09.

The data on the several units, considering the scores in all cities combined, indicate that the greatest per cent of superiority of the experimental over the control groups existed in the case of String Choir. This per cent of superiority is 42. The per cents of superiority of the experimental over the control groups in the remaining units are as follows: Percussion Group, 37; Woodwind Choir, 33; and Brass Choir, 20. These superiorities in mean gains of the experimental over the control groups are all statistically significant; critical ratios range from 6.56 to 13.55.

The differences in mean gains for the picture-unit items of the total music tests were greater for the experimental group in each city. The percentage of superiority was greatest for City B—94 per cent—and least in City A—11 per cent.

The difference in mean gain for the total music picture-unit items of Cities A, B, C, and D combined was 31 points, or 31 per cent greater for the experimental groups than for the control groups. The critical ratio of this difference is 10.65.

TABLE VIII

GAINS MADE BY EXPERIMENTAL AND CONTROL GROUPS ON PICTURE-UNIT ITEMS
MUSIC TESTS

UNIT	A Exp.	A Cont.	B Exp.	B Cont.	C Exp.	C Cont.	D Exp.	D Cont.	E Exp.	E Cont.	Combined Cities Exp.	Combined Cities Cont.
String Choir												
No. of cases	93	92	33	23	100	121	126	123	110	147	462	506
Mean gain	16.30	17.80	36.90	15.68	24.12	17.40	26.76	22.04	24.42	12.34	24.24	17.06
Critical ratio		1.09	10.22		5.42		3.72		11.62		11.05	
% superiority		9.2	135.3		38.6		21.4		97.7		42.1	
Woodwind Choir												
No. of cases	90	93	30	23	102	110	137	127	107	148	466	501
Mean gain	16.18	15.01	36.61	21.10	27.49	18.82	29.26	25.06	23.50	16.66	25.51	19.15
Critical ratio	.88		2.25		6.47		2.84		4.65		8.26	
% superiority	7.8		73.5		46.1		16.8		41.1		33.2	
Brass Choir												
No. of cases	89	83	29	23	101	123	175	120	199	288	593	577
Mean gain	26.92	23.98	45.16	22.00	32.59	26.77	36.43	33.97	27.34	23.59	31.72	26.41
Critical ratio	1.62		10.16		3.71		1.53		2.72		6.56	
% superiority	12.3		105.3		21.7		7.2		15.9		20.1	
Percussion Group												
No. of cases	89	97	31	21	99	120	160	120	148	214	527	572
Mean gain	39.46	27.97	63.82	35.29	46.30	37.81	48.73	31.06	37.33	30.22	44.28	32.32
Critical ratio	4.77		9.57		4.94		10.98		4.44		13.55	
% superiority	41.1		80.8		22.5		56.9		23.5		37.3	
Total Music												
No. of cases	71	77	26	17	85	94	98	93			Cities 280	A to D 281
Mean gain	99.74	89.72	182.78	94.40	130.52	99.62	141.20	109.94			131.30	99.98
Critical ratio	2.14		12.40		7.94		5.95				10.65	
% superiority	11.2		93.6		31.0		28.4				31.3	

TABLE IX

GAINS MADE BY EXPERIMENTAL AND CONTROL GROUPS IN NATURAL SCIENCE AND MUSIC ON NON-PICTURE ITEMS

SUBJECT	CITIES										COMBINED CITIES	
	A		B		C		D		E			
	Exp.	Cont.	Exp.	Cont.	Exp.	Cont.	Exp.	Cont.	Exp.	Cont.	Exp.	Cont.
Total Natural Science												
No. of cases	93	66	68	82	63	79	60	70	81	70	365	367
Mean gain	58.90	57.22	73.96	90.16	69.76	82.12	77.20	55.30	83.38	79.36	72.04	73.18
Critical ratio	.43			4.12		2.83	5.70		1.30			.59
% superiority	2.9			21.9		17.7	39.6		5.1		Cities	1.6 A to D
Total Music												
No. of cases	71	77	26	17	85	94	98	93			280	281
Mean gain	28.30	28.82	56.04	40.38	41.70	32.18	34.56	34.30			37.34	32.46
Critical ratio		.25	4.40		4.28		.14				3.94	
% superiority		1.8	38.8		29.6		0.8				15.0	

In the preceding discussion it has been shown that there was a marked superiority of the experimental over the control groups in mean gains as measured by those items presented both by the talking pictures and by the units of instruction. It is also important to determine whether a superiority in mean gains exists in favor of the control groups on the items included only in the units of instruction.[3] This will be determined in the next section.

TEST ITEMS NOT ANSWERED IN NATURAL SCIENCE PICTURES

Table IX, showing the mean gains of the experimental and control groups in those test items which were not answered either directly or indirectly by the pictures themselves, indicates that in the case of the total natural science tests there was virtually no difference between the two groups in the combined cities. The mean gain in points of the experimental groups was 72 and of the control groups 73. This difference cannot be considered a true difference, the critical ratio being only 0.59. For the music units, the differences in gains made on items which were included in the unit only favored the experimental groups in the total test results in Cities A, B, C, and D combined. The critical ratio, 3.94, indicates a true difference favoring the experimental groups. It seems evident, therefore, that the gains made by the experimental groups, on those items presented both by the picture and by the units, were not made at the expense of the learning of those elements of subject matter which were presented only by the units of instruction.

RESULTS OF COMPLETE FINAL TESTS

It will be remembered that many more items were included in the complete final tests than in the initial tests and Final Tests I in both natural science and music. This was done in order to measure learning over a much wider range of subject matter than was practical with the initial tests. The results of the complete final tests are given in Tables X and XI.

It must be noted that these results do not measure gains over the initial tests, but rather the relative ability of experimental and control groups in all units at the end of each period

[3] It will be remembered that one-fifth of the total class time of the experimental groups was devoted to showing the pictures.

TABLE X

COMPLETE FINAL TEST SCORES MADE BY THE EXPERIMENTAL AND CONTROL GROUPS
NATURAL SCIENCE

UNIT	A Exp.	A Cont.	B Exp.	B Cont.	C Exp.	C Cont.	D Exp.	D Cont.	E Exp.	E Cont.	Combined Exp.	Combined Cont.
Butterflies												
No. of cases	104	78	92	104	76	95	87	82	104	93	463	452
Mean gain	115.25	102.35	130.25	132.25	122.45	123.25	123.00	89.75	139.94	126.15	126.40	116.25
S.D.	32.40	28.67	29.40	30.17	34.29	31.30	25.72	22.52	23.43	26.38	30.45	32.25
Critical ratio	2.84			.47		.14	8.9		3.85		4.88	
% superiority	12.6			1.5		0.7	37.0		10.9		8.7	
Beetles												
No. of cases	100	77	82	101	70	98	85	87	96	97	433	460
Mean gain	104.25	87.10	124.20	118.40	110.45	102.35	104.10	72.65	128.55	112.20	114.45	99.75
S.D.	32.93	27.60	25.45	28.53	30.59	31.63	35.10	23.27	24.65	21.48	31.80	31.61
Critical ratio	3.81		1.45		1.67		6.91		4.91		6.93	
% superiority	19.7		4.9		7.9		43.3		14.6		14.7	
Amphibians												
No. of cases	104	76	84	97	76	95	72	81	102	105	438	454
Mean gain	131.70	120.75	143.70	137.75	125.50	135.55	146.25	108.10	154.80	142.90	140.80	130.05
S.D.	32.33	29.92	25.56	27.47	30.68	27.18	17.46	25.47	16.93	18.01	27.57	28.62
Critical ratio	2.35		1.51			2.24	11.42		4.90		5.78	
% superiority	9.1		4.3			8.0	31.6		8.3		8.3	
Growth of Plants												
No. of cases	107	77	92	104	77	100	88	85	100	108	464	474
Mean gain	88.80	82.35	104.00	111.55	102.05	108.95	104.15	69.60	121.50	103.45	104.15	96.90
S.D.	33.09	28.39	26.38	29.88	26.00	30.81	24.15	22.77	25.54	20.52	29.61	31.14
Critical ratio	1.42			1.63		1.62	9.71		5.61		3.66	
% superiority	7.8			6.2		6.8	49.6		17.4		7.5	
Total Science												
No. of cases	93	66	68	82	63	79	60	70	81	70	365	367
Mean gain	443.45	388.70	516.89	495.50	464.00	463.10	478.55	344.60	551.45	487.10	500.40	438.95
S.D.	126.15	107.27	94.97	109.85	111.65	118.64	78.56	78.84	78.98	68.84	109.35	115.38
Critical ratio	2.95		1.28		.05		9.68		5.35		7.40	
% superiority	14.1		4.3		0.2		38.9		13.2		14.0	

TABLE XI

COMPLETE FINAL TEST SCORES MADE BY THE EXPERIMENTAL AND CONTROL GROUPS

MUSIC

UNIT		A Exp.	A Cont.	B Exp.	B Cont.	C Exp.	C Cont.	D Exp.	D Cont.	E Exp.	E Cont.	Combined Exp.	Combined Cont.
String Choir	No. of cases	93	92	33	23	100	121	126	123	110	147	462	506
	Mean gain	132.31	136.42	149.44	125.44	140.17	129.70	117.22	119.56	135.49	112.39	134.98	123.25
	S.D.	22.29	23.07	16.68	24.26	22.40	24.30	29.82	20.28	17.37	25.04	25.48	25.01
	Critical ratio		1.23	4.12		3.32			.72	8.72		7.20	
	% superiority		3.1	19.1		8.1			2.0	20.6		9.5	
Woodwind Choir	No. of cases	90	93	30	23	102	110	137	127	107	148	466	501
	Mean gain	96.07	91.87	117.70	81.88	107.47	98.45	85.15	89.38	93.79	84.70	96.22	90.22
	S.D.	19.23	20.65	20.13	17.35	20.94	20.32	24.25	18.58	16.71	21.44	22.93	20.88
	Critical ratio	1.42		6.96		3.18			1.60	3.80		4.26	
	% superiority	4.6		43.7		9.2			5.0	10.7		6.7	
Brass Choir	No. of cases	89	83	29	23	101	123	175	120	199	288	593	577
	Mean gain	125.85	105.35	155.75	114.95	130.55	115.30	118.55	113.85	95.80	99.55	115.90	107.30
	S.D.	24.25	26.65	12.45	20.16	23.62	24.25	28.01	23.73	30.65	25.48	31.62	25.90
	Critical ratio	5.26		8.52		4.75		1.55			1.36	5.09	
	% superiority	19.5		35.5		13.2		4.1			3.9	8.0	
Percussion Group	No. of cases	89	97	31	21	99	120	160	120	148	214	527	572
	Mean gain	157.85	132.35	211.55	156.10	174.10	157.75	155.80	132.95	136.20	114.35	157.50	131.95
	S.D.	36.70	33.78	19.64	32.38	36.56	34.26	32.51	35.62	37.95	38.79	39.65	39.79
	Critical ratio	4.91		7.03		3.39		5.52		5.34		10.65	
	% superiority	19.3		35.5		10.4		17.2		19.1		19.4	
Total Music	No. of cases	71	77	26	17	85	94	98	93			Cities 280	A to D 281
	Mean gain	516.66	473.94	632.50	467.86	555.38	499.06	473.62	455.06			524.18	475.70
	S.D.	89.22	83.81	56.82	61.41	84.58	94.13	102.13	82.70			102.08	87.84
	Critical ratio	3.00		8.85		4.22		1.38				6.03	
	% superiority	9.0		35.2		11.3		4.1				10.2	

of experimentation. From these tables it may be seen that achievement in all units, both natural science and music, for the combined cities, was greater for the experimental than for the control groups. It may be seen also that achievement, as measured by the total natural science and music tests, was greater for the experimental than for the control groups. The critical ratios of these differences in achievement, 7.40 in the case of the natural science tests and 6.03 in the music tests, indicate true differences favoring the experimental groups.

SUMMARY OF RESULTS

The results presented in this chapter indicate that the talking pictures used in the experiment made distinct contributions to learning in both natural science and music. The differences in gains for the combined cities were greater for the experimental than for the control groups in the case of every individual unit studied. The critical ratios indicate that differences favoring the experimental groups were statistically significant in every unit in both natural science and music.

A study of the results of the test items, the answers to which were presented both by the talking pictures and by the units of instruction, and which are termed picture-unit items in this study, indicates the specific contribution to learning made by the films. The per cents of superiority of the experimental groups over the control groups for all cities combined on these picture-unit items ranged from 20 to 60 per cent.

It would seem that the specific contribution to learning of the talking picture was determined by the amount of subject matter presented by the film which the classroom teacher did not present as effectively by the use of other methods of subject matter presentation.

In the case of the natural science units, the experimental groups achieved practically as much as the control groups in the subject matter which was presented in the units of instruction and not in the films. In the case of the music units, the experimental groups achieved significantly more than the control groups in this type of subject matter. It would seem, then, that the gains of the experimental over the control groups throughout the experiment were made without sacrificing the learning of subject matter not presented specifically by the films.

CHAPTER IV

EFFECTIVENESS OF THE TALKING PICTURE IN GROUPS OF BELOW AVERAGE AND ABOVE AVERAGE INTELLIGENCE

It was also the purpose of this experiment to determine the effectiveness of the talking picture as a medium of instruction in the teaching of pupils of below average and pupils of above average intelligence. Pupils whose intelligence quotients, as measured by the Pintner Rapid Survey Test, were below 90 were designated as the *low* group; those whose quotients were above 110, as the *high* group.

For the purpose of comparison of achievement in the low and high groups, only the total natural science tests and the total music tests will be considered. Because of the small number of pupils in these low and high intelligence groups, the results from the combined cities only will be considered. In natural science the total number of low intelligence pupils was 113; in music, 113. In natural science the total number of pupils in the high intelligence group was 240; in music, 117.

The test results of the low and high groups will be compared as follows:

1. The final test gains over the initial tests made by the low and high experimental groups will be compared with the gains of their respective control groups.

2. The final test gains in picture-unit items (those items of the tests, the answers to which were furnished both by the pictures and by the units of instruction as discussed in Chapter III) made by the low and high experimental groups will be compared with those made by their respective control groups.

3. The gains in non-picture items (those items of the tests, the answers to which were furnished only by the units of instruction) made by the low and high experimental groups will be compared with those made by their respective control groups.

4. A comparison will be made between the superiority of the

low experimental group over the low control group and the superiority of the high experimental group over the high control group.

TEST RESULTS OF LOW AND HIGH INTELLIGENCE GROUPS IN NATURAL SCIENCE

Table XII gives the test results of the low and high intelligence groups in natural science. It shows that the mean intelligence quotients of the low experimental and control groups were each approximately 81. The mean intelligence quotients of the high experimental and control groups were 121 and 122, respectively. The differences in intelligence quotients of the experimental and control groups are not statistically significant. It can also be seen that the differences in the results of the initial tests in natural science, while favoring the control classes in both the low and high intelligence groups, are not statistically significant.

Final Test Gains Over Initial Tests in Natural Science

Table XII shows that the superiority in mean gains of the low experimental over the low control group was 36.0 points. This difference is statistically significant, the critical ratio being 3.51. In the case of the high groups, the difference between the mean gains favoring the experimental group was 25.04. The critical ratio of this difference is 4.64. The per cent of superiority of the low experimental over the low control group was 37.2; of the high experimental over the high control group, 14.4.

Gains on Picture-Unit Items in Natural Science

The gains made on those items of the tests which were presented by the pictures and also by the units of instruction favored the experimental groups of both low and high intelligence levels. In the case of the low group this difference was 32.2; critical ratio, 5.22. In the case of the high group this difference was 30.65; critical ratio, 9.34. The per cents of superiority of the low and the high experimental groups were 66.9 and 35.5, respectively.

Gains on Non-Picture Items in Natural Science

The differences in the mean gains made on those items which were presented only by the units of instruction (non-picture

TABLE XII: NATURAL SCIENCE TEST RESULTS FOR LOW AND HIGH
INTELLIGENCE GROUPS

	Low I.Q. Groups (Below 90)		High I.Q. Groups (Above 110)	
	Experimental	Control	Experimental	Control
Number of Cases	50	63	130	110
Intelligence Quotient				
Mean	81.20	80.71	121.38	122.30
Difference between means	.49			.92
Critical ratio	.34			.68
Per cent superiority	0.6			0.8
Initial Test				
Mean	79.22	81.34	110.35	115.25
Difference between means		2.12		4.90
Critical ratio		.52		1.39
Per cent superiority		2.7		4.4
Gains Over Initial Test				
Mean	132.82	96.82	198.34	173.30
Difference between means	36.00		25.04	
Critical ratio	3.51		4.64	
Per cent superiority	37.2		14.4	
Gains on Picture-Unit Items				
Mean	80.30	48.10	116.95	86.30
Difference between means	32.20		30.65	
Critical ratio	5.22		9.34	
Per cent superiority	66.9		35.5	
Gains on Non-Picture Items				
Mean	50.22	49.62	83.30	88.06
Difference between means	.60			4.76
Critical ratio	.13			1.74
Per cent superiority	1.2			5.7

TABLE XIII: RELATIVE SUPERIORITY IN MEAN GAINS OF EXPERIMENTAL
GROUPS OVER CONTROL OF HIGH AND LOW INTELLIGENCE–NATURAL SCIENCE

	Low I.Q. Group	High I.Q. Group
Superiority in mean gains of experimental group	36.00	25.04
S.D. of difference in mean gains	10.24	5.40
Difference in superiority in mean gains (superiority of low I.Q. minus superiority of high I.Q.)	10.96	
S.D. of difference in superiority	11.58	
Critical ratio	.95	

items) while, on the one hand, favoring the low experimental pupils, and, on the other hand, the high control pupils, were not statistically significant.

Relative Superiority of Experimental Over Control Groups in Mean Gains in Natural Science

Table XIII shows the relative superiority of low and high intelligence groups in natural science. The superiority in mean gains of the low experimental group over the low control group was 36.00 points. This superiority in the case of the high experimental group was 25.04 points. This difference in superiority of 10.96 (36.00—25.04), in favor of the low intelligence group, is not statistically significant, the critical ratio being 0.95.

The data in Tables XII and XIII indicate that there was a statistically significant difference in mean gains favoring the experimental groups of both the low and the high intelligence levels. While this superiority of the experimental groups seems to be greater in the case of the low intelligence level, it is not sufficiently great to be statistically significant.

TEST RESULTS OF LOW AND HIGH INTELLIGENCE GROUPS IN MUSIC

Table XIV gives the test results of the low and high intelligence groups in music. It shows that the differences between the mean intelligent quotients of the low and high experimental and control groups are not statistically significant. In the initial tests the control groups were favored in the case of the pupils of both low and high intelligence. These differences, however, are not statistically significant.

Final Test Gains Over Initial Tests in Music

Table XIV shows that the difference in the mean gains in the case of the pupils of the low intelligence level was 41.80 points in favor of the experimental over the control group. This difference is statistically significant, the critical ratio being 5.07. The difference between the mean gains of the high intelligence level was 44.50, favoring the experimental group; the critical ratio of this difference is 5.58. The per cents of superiority of the low and high experimental groups were 37.4 and 31.6, respectively.

TABLE XIV: MUSIC TEST RESULTS FOR LOW AND HIGH INTELLIGENCE
QUOTIENT GROUPS

	Low I.Q. Groups (Below 90)		High I.Q. Groups (Above 110)	
	Experimental	Control	Experimental	Control
Number of Cases	67	46	54	63
Intelligence Quotient				
Mean	81.85	84.11	118.20	117.41
Difference between means		2.26	.79	
Critical ratio		2.79	.84	
Per cent superiority		2.8	0.7	
Initial Test				
Mean	96.78	105.50	153.50	169.26
Difference between means		8.72	15.76	
Critical ratio		1.44	2.14	
Per cent superiority		9.0	10.3	
Gains Over Initial Test				
Mean	153.60	111.80	185.40	140.90
Difference between means	41.80		44.50	
Critical ratio	5.07		5.58	
Per cent superiority	37.4		31.6	
Gains on Picture-Unit Items				
Mean	123.10	86.15	141.10	103.81
Difference between means	36.95		37.29	
Critical ratio	5.85		6.51	
Per cent superiority	42.9		35.9	
Gains on Non-Picture Items				
Mean	31.66	28.76	44.06	33.64
Difference between means	2.90		10.42	
Critical ratio	1.11		3.57	
Per cent superiority	10.1		31.0	

TABLE XV: RELATIVE SUPERIORITY IN MEAN GAINS OF EXPERIMENTAL
GROUPS OVER CONTROL OF HIGH AND LOW INTELLIGENCE—MUSIC

	Low I.Q. Group	High I.Q. Group
Superiority in mean gains of experimental group	41.80	44.50
S.D. of difference in mean gains	8.24	7.98
Difference in superiority in mean gains (superiority of high I.Q. minus superiority of low I.Q.)		2.70
S.D. of difference in superiority		11.47
Critical ratio		.23

Gains on Picture-Unit Items in Music

The gains made on the picture-unit items of the test were greater for the experimental groups of both low and high intelligence. The superiority in mean gains of the low experimental over the low control group was 36.95. This superiority in the case of the high experimental over the high control group was 37.29. The critical ratios of these differences were 5.85 and 6.51, respectively. The per cents of superiority were 42.9 in the case of the low experimental group and 35.9 in the case of the high experimental group.

It is interesting to note that the mean gain made by the *low experimental* group on these picture-unit items was 123.10 points and that made by the *high control* group was 103.81 points. This difference in gains favoring the low experimental group (19.29) may be considered a statistically significant difference, the critical ratio being 3.61. It represents a 19 per cent superiority.

Gains on Non-Picture Items in Music

The gains made on the non-picture items of the test favored the experimental groups in the case of the pupils of both low and high intelligence. This difference is not statistically significant in the case of the low experimental group. The difference in gains on these items favoring the high experimental group, however, is statistically significant, the critical ratio being 3.57. The per cents of superiority of the low and the high experimental groups were 10.1 and 31.0, respectively.

Relative Superiority of Experimental Over Control Groups in Mean Gains in Music

Table XV shows that the superiority in mean gains made by the low experimental group was 41.80 points; that made by the high experimental group, 44.50 points. The difference in superiority was 2.70, favoring the high intelligence level. This difference is not statistically significant, the critical ratio being only .23.

The data in Tables XIV and XV indicate that there was a statistically significant difference in mean gains favoring the experimental classes of both the low and the high intelligence levels. While this superiority in music seems to be greater in the case of the high intelligence level, it is not statistically significant.

SUMMARY

From the evidence furnished by the test results in the case of both the natural science and music units, it appears that these educational sound films make a distinct contribution to the learning of pupils of both low and high intelligence levels.

CHAPTER V

RESULTS OF RECALL TESTS

IN THIS chapter the recall test results made by the experimental groups will be compared with those made by the control groups in the natural science and music units of instruction. Comparisons will be in terms of gains made on the recall test over the initial test, gains made on the picture-unit items of the recall test, gains made on the non-picture items of the recall test, and the per cent of the final test retained on the recall test.

The recall test items were identical with those of the initial tests given two weeks prior to the beginning of the experimental teaching. The recall tests were administered in the same manner as were the other tests of the experiment, four weeks after the completion of the final unit of instruction, or ten weeks after the completion of the first unit of the experiment.

RECALL TEST GAINS OVER INITIAL TESTS
IN NATURAL SCIENCE

The recall test gains over the initial tests made by the experimental and control groups in natural science are given in Table XVI. This table shows that the total recall test gains in natural science for the combined cities favored the experimental group. The total mean gain for the experimental group was 128.50 points, and for the control group, 111.14 points, indicating a superiority of 15.6 per cent in favor of the experimental group. The critical ratio of the difference between the means of the two groups is 4.65, indicating a difference that is statistically significant.

The per cents of superiority for the individual units were: Butterflies, 9.4; Beetles, 18.3; Amphibians, 15.9; and Growth of Plants, 11.4. The critical ratios of the differences between the means of both groups were 2.88, 4.42, 4.59, and 2.71 for each of the four units, respectively. The first and last of these critical ratios are not statistically significant.

TABLE XVI

RECALL TEST GAINS OVER INITIAL TEST MADE BY EXPERIMENTAL AND CONTROL GROUPS

NATURAL SCIENCE

UNIT	A Exp.	A Cont.	B Exp.	B Cont.	C Exp.	C Cont.	D Exp.	D Cont.	E Exp.	E Cont.	Combined Exp.	Combined Cont.
Butterflies												
No. of cases	96	73	81	86	71	87	76	77	95	85	419	408
Mean gain	30.05	22.85	33.11	32.00	29.84	34.37	33.71	27.14	37.04	32.42	32.87	30.05
Critical ratio	3.67		.49			2.04	3.17		2.19		2.88	
% superiority	31.5		3.5			30.4	24.2		14.3		9.4	
Beetles												
No. of cases	94	71	73	81	66	88	76	80	89	90	398	410
Mean gain	27.00	15.04	31.28	30.74	21.28	24.04	26.08	18.58	29.32	25.14	27.18	22.98
Critical ratio	6.72		.25			1.22	3.33		2.52		4.42	
% superiority	79.5		1.8			13.0	40.4		16.6		18.3	
Amphibians												
No. of cases	97	69	77	80	71	86	75	82	96	98	416	415
Mean gain	32.08	24.61	32.80	29.05	27.40	26.71	39.19	27.85	35.02	34.12	33.37	28.78
Critical ratio	3.47		1.88		.30		5.15		.42		4.59	
% superiority	30.4		12.9		2.6		40.7		2.6		15.9	
Growth of Plants												
No. of cases	99	70	84	88	72	92	81	81	95	102	431	433
Mean gain	31.36	28.87	31.81	39.70	33.37	31.78	32.26	20.38	38.41	28.93	33.52	30.10
Critical ratio	.78		2.72		.56		4.95		4.86		2.71	
% superiority	8.6		24.8		5.0		58.3		32.8		11.4	
Total Science												
No. of cases	86	60	63	71	61	74	55	66	76	64	341	335
Mean gain	120.10	88.10	134.42	128.66	114.42	115.62	134.50	98.90	140.18	120.66	128.50	111.14
Critical ratio	4.04		.66		.15		4.21		2.71		4.65	
% superiority	36.3		4.5		1.0		36.0		16.2		15.6	

TABLE XVII

RECALL TEST GAINS OVER INITIAL TEST MADE BY EXPERIMENTAL AND CONTROL GROUPS
MUSIC

UNIT	CITIES A		B		C		D		E		COMBINED CITIES	
	Exp.	Cont.	Exp.	Cont.	Exp.	Cont.	Exp.	Cont.	Exp.	Cont.	Exp.	Cont.
String Choir												
No. of cases	83	85	27	20	94	115	117	116	70	138	391	474
Mean gain	17.50	20.80	52.46	20.80	30.52	22.28	29.50	26.68	29.82	18.90	28.84	22.04
Critical ratio		1.73	17.49		5.49		1.67		7.05		7.47	
% superiority		18.9	152.2		37.0		10.6		57.8		30.9	
Woodwind Choir												
No. of cases	82	87	26	21	96	105	126	120	65	142	395	475
Mean gain	20.89	25.39	47.38	24.43	30.91	23.74	34.78	32.14	35.74	23.38	31.96	26.08
Critical ratio		2.10	5.68		3.60		1.33		5.59		5.55	
% superiority		21.6	93.9		30.2		8.2		52.9		22.5	
Brass Choir												
No. of cases	79	78	26	22	98	117	126	116	128	213	457	546
Mean gain	24.98	21.47	45.38	23.27	29.96	24.17	29.51	30.50	29.33	26.60	29.69	26.03
Critical ratio	1.46		6.34		3.23			.50	1.55		3.73	
% superiority	16.3		95.0		23.1			3.4	10.3		14.1	
Percussion Group												
No. of cases	77	92	28	19	97	116	114	116	140	204	456	547
Mean gain	39.78	27.81	64.59	39.33	46.95	41.19	43.68	33.45	39.27	29.94	43.65	33.03
Critical ratio	4.16		6.38		2.28		4.26		4.60		8.70	
% superiority	43.0		64.2		14.0		30.6		31.2		32.2	
Tota. Music												
No. of cases	64	72	23	16	84	91	92	90			Cities 263	A to D 269
Mean gain	104.50	97.50	209.70	108.98	139.78	108.50	134.74	122.58			134.02	110.02
Critical ratio	.89		10.47		5.46		1.67				5.77	
% superiority	7.2		92.4		28.8		9.9				21.8	

RECALL TEST GAINS OVER INITIAL TESTS
IN MUSIC

Table XVII gives the recall test gains over the initial tests for the music units. It shows that the mean gains made by the experimental groups in all cities combined exceeded the mean gains made by the control groups in every unit studied. Each of these differences is statistically significant, the critical ratios ranging from 3.73 to 8.70. The per cents of superiority favoring the experimental groups for the individual units in the music series were: String Choir, 30.9; Woodwind Choir, 22.5; Brass Choir, 14.1; and Percussion Group, 32.2.

The mean gain made by the experimental group for the combined cities A, B, C, and D[1] exceeded that made by the control group in the total recall test in music by 21.8 per cent. The critical ratio of this difference is 5.77, indicating a true superiority of the experimental group.

RECALL TEST GAINS ON PICTURE-UNIT ITEMS

Table XVIII gives the recall test gains in natural science made by experimental and control groups on those items, the answers to which were furnished either directly or indirectly by both the pictures and the units of instruction. The purpose of this section is to compare these results in order to secure a partial indication of the specific contribution of the talking picture to the units studied.

The table shows that the difference in mean gains made by the experimental and control groups of the combined cities favored the experimental groups in the case of every unit studied. The critical ratios indicate that these differences are all statistically significant. The per cents of superiority of experimental over control groups for the individual units were Butterflies, 29.2; Beetles, 44.1; Amphibians, 27.1; and Growth of Plants, 41.4.

For the total natural science test the mean gain made by the experimental groups on the picture-unit items exceeded (by 37.2 per cent) that made by the control groups for all cities combined. The difference in mean gains favoring the experimental groups is statistically significant, the critical ratio being 9.00.

---

[1] It will be recalled that because of administrative difficulties, the classes of City E could participate in only two of the units of the experiment. See Chapter III, page 26.

TABLE XVIII

RECALL TEST GAINS MADE BY EXPERIMENTAL AND CONTROL GROUPS ON PICTURE-UNIT ITEMS
NATURAL SCIENCE

| UNIT | CITIES | | | | | | | | | | COMBINED CITIES | |
| | A | | B | | C | | D | | E | | | |
	Exp.	Cont.	Exp.	Cont.	Exp.	Cont.	Exp.	Cont.	Exp.	Cont.	Exp.	Cont.
Butterflies												
No. of cases	96	73	81	86	71	87	76	77	95	85	419	408
Mean gain	18.68	11.84	20.58	16.64	18.30	15.88	19.86	13.48	20.36	17.26	19.58	15.16
Critical ratio	4.75		2.88		1.79		5.06		2.58		7.49	
% superiority	57.8		23.7		15.2		27.3		18.0		29.2	
Beetles												
No. of cases	94	71	73	81	66	88	76	80	89	90	398	410
Mean gain	19.12	8.78	20.94	18.26	15.28	12.64	15.48	8.32	18.72	13.92	18.04	12.52
Critical ratio	7.89		1.77		1.66		4.90		4.00		8.49	
% superiority	117.8		14.7		20.9		86.1		34.5		44.1	
Amphibians												
No. of cases	97	69	77	80	71	86	75	82	96	98	416	415
Mean gain	24.82	17.44	23.47	19.60	20.95	17.89	28.93	19.66	25.87	19.15	24.88	19.57
Critical ratio	4.22		2.36		1.65		5.62		3.61		6.81	
% superiority	42.3		19.7		17.1		47.2		35.1		27.1	
Growth of Plants												
No. of cases	99	70	84	88	72	92	81	81	95	102	431	433
Mean gain	17.89	14.56	14.65	16.51	14.14	9.91	13.84	6.52	17.92	9.25	15.88	11.23
Critical ratio	1.60		.97		2.30		3.83		4.93		5.34	
% superiority	22.9		12.7		42.7		112.27		93.7		41.4	
Total Science												
No. of cases	86	60	63	71	61	74	55	66	76	64	341	335
Mean gain	79.66	49.90	82.70	70.22	69.90	54.86	79.74	50.38	83.26	62.62	79.34	57.82
Critical ratio	5.41		2.24		2.77		5.64		4.35		9.00	
% superiority	59.6		17.8		27.4		58.3		33.0		37.2	

TABLE XIX

RECALL TEST GAINS MADE BY THE EXPERIMENTAL AND THE CONTROL GROUPS ON PICTURE-UNIT ITEMS

MUSIC

| UNIT | CITIES | | | | | | | | | | COMBINED CITIES | |
	A Exp.	A Cont.	B Exp.	B Cont.	C Exp.	C Cont.	D Exp.	D Cont.	E Exp.	E Cont.	Exp.	Cont.
Strings												
No. of cases	83	85	27	20	94	115	117	116	70	138	391	474
Mean gain	14.16	15.34	37.32	14.30	22.98	15.90	23.22	20.04	23.30	13.18	21.76	15.96
Critical ratio		.85	11.12		5.85		2.41		7.97		8.06	
% superiority		8.3	161.0		44.5		15.9		76.8		36.3	
Woodwinds												
No. of cases	82	87	26	21	96	105	126	120	65	142	395	475
Mean gain	14.64	16.84	33.42	16.22	22.08	16.70	24.36	21.96	24.56	15.00	22.42	17.52
Critical ratio		1.26	2.95		3.56		1.64		5.56		6.12	
% superiority		15.0	106.0		32.2		10.9		63.7		27.9	
Brasses												
No. of cases	79	78	26	22	98	117	126	116	128	213	457	546
Mean gain	20.40	17.80	36.04	17.40	25.16	20.08	25.62	26.46	24.96	22.08	25.02	21.78
Critical ratio	1.24		5.22		3.22			.47	1.93		3.76	
% superiority	14.6		107.1		25.3			3.3	13.0		14.9	
Percussion												
No. of cases	77	92	28	19	97	116	114	116	140	204	456	547
Mean gain	31.87	24.25	52.87	32.26	32.63	31.51	37.54	25.93	29.98	25.21	35.80	26.77
Critical ratio	3.22		6.17		3.11		5.86		2.68		9.21	
% superiority	31.4		63.9		19.4		44.8		18.9		33.7	
Total Music											Cities	A to D
No. of cases	64	72	23	16	84	91	92	90			263	269
Mean	81.66	72.50	159.50	81.50	108.54	81.82	109.70	93.98			106.54	84.54
Critical ratio	1.39		10.97		6.23		2.77				6.16	
% superiority	12.6		95.7		32.6		16.7				26.0	

The recall test gains made by both the experimental group and the control group on picture-unit items in music are given in Table XIX.

It may be seen from this table that for all cities combined the experimental groups exceeded the control groups in mean gains made on the recall tests in each of the music units. The critical ratios indicate that for every unit the differences favoring the experimental group are statistically significant. The per cents of superiority of experimental over control groups for the several music units ranged from 15 in the case of Brass Choir, to 36 in the case of String Choir. For the total music test the mean gain made by the experimental group of the combined cities exceeded that of the control group by 26.0 per cent. This difference favoring the experimental group is statistically significant, the critical ratio being 6.16.

RECALL TEST GAINS ON NON-PICTURE ITEMS

Table XX gives the recall test gains made by experimental and control groups on non-picture items in natural science and music. By non-picture items is meant those items the answers to which were furnished only by the units of instruction and which were answered neither directly nor indirectly by the pictures. The purpose of this section is to determine whether the significant gains made by the experimental groups on the picture-unit items were made at the expense of the elements of subject matter which were presented only by the various units of instruction.

The table shows that in the total natural science test the mean gain made by the control group for the combined cities on non-picture items exceeded that made by the experimental group, but that the experimental group made the greater mean gain in the total music test. Neither of these differences in mean gains was sufficiently great to be statistically significant. The critical ratios were 2.26 in natural science and 2.17 in music. It would seem, therefore, that the greater recall test gains made by the experimental groups were not made at the expense of elements of subject matter presented only by the units of instruction. A similar conclusion was reached (see Chapter III) in regard to the greater gains in *learning* made by the experimental groups, as measured by the final tests.

TABLE XX

RECALL TEST GAINS MADE BY EXPERIMENTAL AND CONTROL GROUPS ON NON-PICTURE ITEMS IN NATURAL SCIENCE AND MUSIC

| SUBJECT | CITIES | | | | | | | | | | COMBINED CITIES | |
| | A | | B | | C | | D | | E | | | |
	Exp.	Cont.	Exp.	Cont.	Exp.	Cont.	Exp.	Cont.	Exp.	Cont.	Exp.	Cont.
Total Science												
No. of cases	86	60	63	71	61	74	55	66	76	64	341	335
Mean gain	40.85	38.65	51.35	58.40	44.40	60.30	54.65	48.05	56.75	57.00	49.20	53.00
Critical ratio	.70			1.87		4.60	1.64			.08		2.26
% superiority	5.7			13.7		35.8	13.7			0.4		7.7
Total Music												
No. of cases	64	72	23	16	84	91	92	90			263	269
Mean gain	22.58	21.90	49.66	28.26	32.26	26.74	25.70	29.10			29.14	26.30
Critical ratio	.27		5.13		2.63			1.66			2.17	
% superiority	3.1		75.7		20.6			13.23			10.8	

PER CENT OF RETENTION FROM FINAL TEST

The foregoing discussion has been concerned with the gains over the initial test made by the experimental and control groups on the recall tests. This section will consider the amounts of the final test gains retained by the experimental and control groups as measured by the recall tests. These amounts of retention will be expressed in terms of percentage. For instance, suppose a pupil made a total gain of 100 on the final test over the initial test. It may be assumed that he has *learned* one hundred units of the test. Now suppose that on the recall test given several weeks later, he showed a gain over the initial test of only 80. It may be assumed that he has retained only eighty units of the test which he learned and could answer at the time of the final test. This amount of retention shall be considered to be 80 per cent. However, if on the recall test he made a gain of 120 over his initial test score it may be assumed that there has been additional learning on his part subsequent to the final test. Where this has occurred it can not be said that he has retained 120 per cent of what he had learned to the time the final test was given. In the cases where this situation existed the pupil was credited with perfect retention or, in other words, he was assigned a percentage of retention of 100.

The experimental and control groups for all cities combined were compared with respect to mean per cents of retention of the final test, as measured by the recall test. Results in natural science and music are given in Table XXI.

This table shows that the experimental groups exceeded the control groups in the mean per cent of information retained from

TABLE XXI

MEAN PER CENTS OF RETENTION OF FINAL TEST IN RECALL TEST—
TOTAL NATURAL SCIENCE AND MUSIC UNITS FOR ALL CITIES
COMBINED

	NATURAL SCIENCE		MUSIC	
	Exp.	Cont.	Exp.	Cont.
Number of cases	338	335	262	268
Mean per cent	69.86	66.62	78.35	81.02
Critical ratio	2.49			1.68
Per cent superiority	4.9			3.4

the final test in the case of the natural science units and that the control groups exceeded the experimental groups in the mean per cent of information retained from the final tests in the case of the music units. These differences are slight, however, and are not statistically significant in either the natural science or the music units; the critical ratios of these differences are 2.49 in the case of natural science and 1.68 in the case of music. From these data it seems, therefore, that there is no significant difference between the amounts of learning retained by the experimental or the control groups in natural science or music.

SUMMARY

From the data given in this chapter it appears that the talking pictures used in this experiment made a lasting contribution to learning in both natural science and music. The differences in gains favored the experimental groups for the combined cities in the total recall tests and were statistically significant.

In the items of the tests the answers to which were presented both by the pictures and by the units of instruction, the mean gains of the experimental groups exceeded in a marked degree those of the control groups in the case of every unit studied, both in natural science and in music. These differences in gains favoring the experimental groups were statistically significant.

These statistically significant differences in mean recall test gains of the experimental groups appear not to have been made at the expense of the learning of subject matter presented only by the units of instruction. This conclusion seems to be justified by the data on the comparison of the experimental and control groups on the non-picture items of the tests. The differences in mean gains made by the experimental and control groups on these items were not statistically significant for either natural science or music.

CHAPTER VI

EFFECTIVENESS OF SPECIFIC ELEMENTS OF
PICTURE COMPOSITION OF THE FILMS
USED IN THE EXPERIMENT

This chapter is concerned with the effectiveness of certain technical elements of sound film composition which lend themselves to objective analysis. More general elements of picture composition such as the introduction, the treatment of objectives, the unique use of the medium, and correlation with important concepts not developed in the picture are highly important in themselves, but can not be treated in the present study. These elements relate more to the technical preparation of the sound film as distinguished from its educational aspects.

The determination of the relative effectiveness of these technical elements of composition is fundamental to the future production of talking pictures for classroom use. The talking picture as an instructional medium offers a wide range of composition elements in the presentation of all types of subject matter. A few of these elements are: type of photography such as slow motion, time lapse, animation, and natural; focal length such as close-up, medium, and long; length of scene; quality of lighting; time of occurrence in film; types of sound; repetition of scenes; and integration of sight and sound.

The production of classroom films is usually based upon the subjective opinion of directors who may or may *not* have had actual contact with classroom situations or with the educational philosophy and psychology underlying modern classroom practice. In any case it is possible that traditional methods of talking picture production may not be the most effective in the actual presentation of subject materials.

It must be remembered that all these elements of composition involve not only pictorial and sound elements as such, but also an adequate integration of each with the other in order to realize to the greatest possible extent the educational possibilities

[continued on p. 70]

55

TABLE XXII

ANALYSIS OF COMPOSITION ELEMENTS USED IN THE FILMS

TEST ITEM	TYPE OF PHOTOGRAPHY	FOCAL LENGTH	SCENE LENGTH	QUALITY OF LIGHT	SPEECH OR OTHER SOUND	MINUTE IN PICTURE	INTEGRATION OF SOUND AND SCENE	REPETITION
				HIGHEST QUARTER				
The butterfly comes out of the chrysalis 1. tail first 2. head first	Natural	Close-up " "	20" 23"	Excellent "	Speech "	4½ 8	Excellent	Yes
The caterpillar eats the shell of the egg from which it is hatched. (T-F)*	Natural	Close-up " "	9" 6"	Very good Excellent	Speech "	2 7	Excellent	Yes
In primitive music, such as that of the Indians, the percussion instrument usually employed is 1. bass drum 2. tambourine 3. tom tom 4. tympani.	Natural	Medium	20"	Excellent	Speech and sound	8½	Excellent	No
At night the tiger beetle 1. gets its food 2. seeks shelter.	Natural	Medium	12"	Fair	Speech	5	Excellent	No
The United States government is making a great effort and spending much money in trying to control the Japanese beetles. (T-F)	Natural and animated	Long shot	60"	Good	Speech	5–6	Excellent	Yes
The tongue of the toad is fastened to the mouth 1. at the back 2. at the front.	Natural and slow motion	Close-up	30"	Very good	Speech	6	Excellent	Yes

Question							
Which one of the following is unusually struck with one stick or hammer? 1. Chimes 2. Xylophone 3. Bells 4. Tambourine	Natural	Close-up	40"	Excellent	Speech and sound	1	Good	Yes
The eggs of the swallow-tail butterfly are laid 1. in clusters 2. in a row 3. singly 4. in two rows.	Natural	Close-up	7"	Excellent	Speech	6	Excellent	No
The tiger beetle larva holds itself in place by 1. a silken thread 2. two humps on its back 3. a sticky substance 4. its strong jaws.	Natural	Close-up	12"	Excellent	Speech	2	Excellent	Yes
The number of tones the double bass usually plays lower than the cello is: 1. four 2. eight 3. twelve 4. sixteen.	Natural	Medium	20"	Fair	Speech and duet	2	Good	Yes
After the butterfly has come out of the chrysalis its wings grow to their full strength and size in about 1. a minute 2. an hour 3. a day 4. a week.	Stop motion / Natural	Medium / Close-up	25" / 23"	Very good / Excellent	Speech / "	4½ / 9	Excellent	Yes

* T–F = True-False, E–C = Essay-Completion.

TABLE XXII (*Continued*)

TEST ITEM	TYPE OF PHOTOGRAPHY	FOCAL LENGTH	SCENE LENGTH	QUALITY OF LIGHT	SPEECH OR OTHER SOUND	MINUTE IN PICTURE	INTEGRATION OF SOUND AND SCENE	REPETITION
The number of trombones commonly used in the symphony orchestra is about 1. one 2. three or four 3. eight or nine 4. twelve.	Natural	Medium Close-up	20″	Good Excellent	Speech Speech and sound	8	Good	Yes
The number of French horns commonly used in the symphony orchestra is——.	Natural	Medium Long shot Close up	10″ 10″ 30″	Good " Very good	Speech and sound Sound "	4 4½ 4½	Good	Yes
The chief purpose of the double bass is to 1. emphasize climaxes 2. play bass solos 3. re-enforce the bass tones of the harmony 4. repeat the keynote only at regular intervals.	Natural	Close-up	40″	Excellent	Speech and sound	[9	Excellent	Yes
The French horn is held in the same manner as the tuba. (T-F).	Natural	Close-up		Excellent	Picture alone		Good	Yes
The chrysalis 1. opens at one end 2. splits open along the back when the butterfly comes out.	Natural	Close-up "	20″ 20″	Excellent "	Speech "	4½ 8	Excellent	Yes
Bees in visiting flowers accidentally get pollen on their bodies. (T-F)	Natural " "	Close-up " " "	60″ 29″ 15″ 16″	Excellent Very good Good "	Speech " " "	4-5½ " "	Excellent	Yes

Item								
The number of French horns commonly used in the symphony orchestra is about 1. one 2. three or four 3. eight or nine 4. twelve.	Natural	Medium / Close-up	10" / 30"	Good / Excellent	Speech and sound / Speech	5-6	Good	Yes
The player of the double bass 1. sits 2. stands while playing.	Natural	Close-up	40"	Excellent	Sound and picture	9	Good	Yes
Frog's eggs are 1. light in color. 2. dark in color.	Natural	Close-up	25"	Excellent	Speech	1	Excellent	Yes
The snare drum often marks the 1. beat 2. after beat.	Natural	Medium	5" / 10"	Good	Speech and sound	7½ 7½	Excellent	Yes
An octave is —— tones lower or higher than a given tone.	Natural	Medium	10" / 10"	Good	Speech "	2½ 2½	Good	No
Tadpoles look like ...... (E-C)	Natural	Close-up / Close-up	10" plus other scenes	Excellent / Very good	Speech	1-2	Excellent	Yes
Tiger beetles are found where the soil is —— and ——.	Natural	Medium	7"	Good	Speech	1	Poor	No
The —— has a metal crook at the top and a gourd-like bell at the bottom.	Natural	Close-up	30"	Excellent	Speech and sound	6½	Excellent	Yes

TABLE XXII (Continued)

TEST ITEM	TYPE OF PHOTOGRAPHY	FOCAL LENGTH	SCENE LENGTH	QUALITY OF LIGHT	SPEECH OR OTHER SOUND	MINUTE IN PICTURE	INTEGRATION OF SOUND AND SCENE	RE-PETITION
The cello is held by the player in the same manner as the viola. (T-F)	Natural	Medium	20"	Excellent	Speech and sound	3	Good	Yes
		Close-up	30"	"	Speech and sound	5		
The tone quality of the tuba is ———.	Natural	Medium	10"	Good	Speech	9	Excellent	Yes
		"	30"	Excellent	Sound	9		
Man's first musical instrument was probably some form of 1. tympani 2. xylophone 3. drum 4. chimes.	Natural	Close-up	10"	Excellent	Speech	7	Excellent	No
		Medium	20"	"	Sound	7		
The place where the tiger beetle pupa passes the pupal stage is ...... (E-C)	Natural	Close-up	100"	Good	Speech	2-3	Excellent	Yes
One place where the ichneumon fly may lay her eggs is ...... (E-C)	Natural	Close-up	13"	Good	Speech	5½	Excellent	Yes
		"	15"	Excellent	Picture alone	5½	"	"
Tiger beetle larvae feed on 1. fruits 2. roots of plants 3. leaves of plants 4. insects.	Natural	Close-up	12"	Good	Speech	2	Excellent	Yes
		"	11"	Excellent	"	2		
		"	7"	"	Picture alone	2		
		"	11"	"	"	2		

Question								
The cello may play either bass or tenor. (T-F)	Natural	Medium	15″	Good	Speech and sound	6	Excellent	No
Which one of the following percussion instruments is played in much the same manner as the piano? 1. Celesta 2. Chimes 3. Bells 4. Xylophone	Natural	Medium	40″	Good	Speech and sound	4	Good	No
The largest woodwind instrument is the 1. English horn 2. clarinet 3. bassoon 4. flute.	Natural	Close-up " "		Very good "	Picture* alone		Goo	Yes
The second violin is 1. the same size as 2. larger than the first violin.	Natural	Close-up	20″	Fair	Speech	3	Poor	Yes
When a plant seed begins to grow, it sends a root 1. upward 2. downward.	Time-lapse	Close-up	22″ 17″	Excellent	Speech "	1 1	Excellent	Yes
Brass wire, spun into shape and then hammered, is used to make the 1. cymbals 2. castanets 3. gong 4. tympani.	Natural	Close-up	10″	Excellent	Speech	7	Good	No

* Throughout mostly last 4.

TABLE XXII (*Continued*)

TEST ITEM	TYPE OF PHOTOG-RAPHY	FOCAL LENGTH	SCENE LENGTH	QUALITY OF LIGHT	SPEECH OR OTHER SOUND	MINUTE IN PICTURE	INTEGRATION OF SOUND AND SCENE	RE-PETI-TION
Three of the following are made chiefly of metal. Which one is *not* made chiefly of metal? 1. Gong 2. Triangle 3. Castanets 4. Cymbals	Natural	Close-up		Excellent	Speech and sound " "		Poor	No
The slide of the trombone is used to · · · (E–C)	Natural	Close-up	40"	Excellent	Sound	7	Good	Yes
The eyes of the tadpole are different from those of the frog because the tadpole's eyes . . . while the frog's eyes . . . (E–C)	Natural	Close-up "	25" 30"	Very good Excellent	Speech "	3 8	Excellent	Yes
The castanets originated among the 1. Spaniards 2. Turks 3. Moors 4. Greeks.	Natural	Medium	30"	Good	Speech	8	Excellent	No
The keel 1. takes in food from the air 2. supports weak stems 3. protects the stamen and pistil 4. takes in moisture from the soil.	Natural	Close-up	35"	Excellent	Speech	3½	Excellent	No
The instrument of the string choir that can produce the lowest tone is the ———.	Natural	Close-up	20" plus 20" for Dem.	Excellent	Speech and sound	9	Good	Yes

Question								
The tadpole's tail drops off just before it becomes a frog. (T-F)	Natural	Medium	35"	Good	Speech	4	Excellent	No
Which one of the following beetles is a friend of man? 1. Ladybird 2. Japanese 3. Rose 4. Corn-borer	Natural	Close-up " "	7" 7"	Fair Excellent	Speech "	8 10	Excellent	Yes
Caterpillars shed their skin every few 1. minutes 2. hours 3. days 4. weeks.	Natural	Close-up	20"	Excellent	Speech	7	Excellent	Yes

LOWEST QUARTER

Question								
The piccolo is much like the —— except that its tone is ——.	Trick and Natural	Medium	20"	Fair	Sound	10	Poor	No
The percussion instrument of the symphony orchestra having bars made of wood is the ——.	Natural	Medium	10"	Good	Speech and sound	3	Excellent	No
The soprano instruments of the woodwind choir are: ——, ——, and ——.	Natural	Close-up Medium	10" {10" 10"	Good Excellent " Good	Speech and sound " "	2 2 3 9	Poor	Yes
The bass drum rarely has the principal rhythmic accent. (T-F)	Natural	Medium	10"	Good		8 8	Excellent	Yes

TABLE XXII (*Continued*)

TEST ITEM	TYPE OF PHOTOG-RAPHY	FOCAL LENGTH	SCENE LENGTH	QUALITY OF LIGHT	SPEECH OR OTHER SOUND	MINUTE IN PICTURE	INTEGRATION OF SOUND AND SCENE	RE-PETI-TION
Bees carry ——— from flower to flower	Natural "	Medium "	60" 16"	Excellent Good	Speech "	4–5½ 4–5½	Excellent	Yes
The number of bass trombones commonly used in the symphony orchestra is ———.	Natural	Medium Close-up	10" 10"	Good	Speech Sound	8½	Good	No
For woodwind music of high pitch and exceptional intensity the ——— is used.	Natural	Medium Close-up	10"	Excellent	Speech and sound	9	Poor	No
Young tadpoles breathe by means of ———.	Natural	Medium Close-up	15"	Excellent	Speech	2	Excellent	No
The tiger beetle is 1. an enemy of man 2. a friend of man.	Natural	Medium	6"	Very good	Speech	2	Poor	Yes
The number of tenor trombones commonly used in the symphony orchestra is ———.	Natural	Medium	20"	Good	Speech	8	Good	No
The tympani 1. must be struck by the hand 2. may be tuned 3. are played with the aid of a keyboard 4. have wooden resonators to enrich the tone	Natural	Medium Medium	10" 10"	Good Good	Speech and sound "	8	Excellent	No
Pitch changes on three of the following instruments are made by having bars of different lengths. Which one does *not* have bars of different lengths? 1. Bells	Natural	Varying focal lengths			Sound " "		Poor	No

2. Triangle
3. Chimes
4. Xylophone

Item	Setting	Shot	Time	Quality	Presentation	No.	Rating	Yes/No
"Kettle drums" is the name often applied to _____ .	Natural	Medium	10"	Good	Speech and sound	4	Good	No
The basses of the brass choir are the _____ and the _____ .	Natural	Medium " Close-up	10" 30"	Good " Excellent	Speech and sound " Sound	7 9 9	Poor	No
In the clarinet, sound is produced by 1. blowing across a hole near one end 2. the vibration of two delicate reed-ends when breath is applied 3. air-forced vibration of a single reed against the mouthpiece 4. the action of the fingers on the keys.	Natural	Medium	10"	Good	Speech and sound	6½	Good	No
In order to grow into new plants, seeds need 1. …… 2. …… 3. …… (E-C)	Time-lapse	Close-up " "	20" 35"	Good "	Speech "	1 10	Poor	Yes
The outer wings of beetles are used as . . . (E-C)	Natural	Medium	24"	Excellent	Speech	10	Good	Yes
Bees visit flowers in order to get 1. minerals 2. oxygen 3. water 4. nectar.	Natural	Close-up Medium " Close-up	60" 29" 15" 16"	Excellent Good " "	Picture alone " " Speech	4-5½ " " "	Poor Excellent Poor	Yes

TABLE XXII (*Continued*)

TEST ITEM	TYPE OF PHOTOGRAPHY	FOCAL LENGTH	SCENE LENGTH	QUALITY OF LIGHT	SPEECH OR OTHER SOUND	MINUTE IN PICTURE	INTEGRATION OF SOUND AND SCENE	REPETITION
Accompanying instruments are played 1. more 2. less prominently than the solo instruments.	Natural				Sound "	2–9	Poor	Yes
The tones of three of the following instruments are considered brilliant. Which one is the *least* brilliant in tone? 1. Xylophone 2. Bells 3. Chimes 4. Triangle	Natural	Close-up Medium Close-up	Various	Excellent Good Excellent	Sound " "	Various	Poor	No
During the playing of string choir selections the position of the conductor is . . . (E-C)	Natural	Medium "		Good "	Picture alone "	1 9	Poor	Yes
The English horn is the alto of the brass choir. (T-F)	Natural	Medium	10"	Good	Speech	5	Good	No
Japanese beetle eggs hatch in about 1. 2 days 2. 15 days 3. 60 days 4. 90 days	Natural	Medium	15"	Poor	Speech	6	Poor	No
The clarinet may play soprano, alto, or tenor parts. (T-F)	Natural	Medium "	15" 15"	Fair "	Speech Sound		Poor	No
The difference between the mouthpiece of the oboe and clarinet is that the mouthpiece of the oboe . . . (E-C)	Natural	Medium Close-up	10" 10"	Excellent "	Speech "	3 4	Good	No

The names of the instruments of the brass choir are . . . (E-C)	Natural	Medium	30″	Excellent	Speech alone	2	Poor	Yes
Percussion instruments are so called because . . . (E-C)	Natural	Medium	10″	Good	Speech alone	1	Poor	No
The bell of the French horn is 1. larger 2. smaller than that of the trombone.	Natural	Close-up Medium "	20″	Good " "	Picture alone " "		Poor	No
The flute is smaller than the piccolo. (T-F)	Natural	Medium	15″	Good	Picture alone		Poor	No
The place where the eggs of the frog are laid is in the ———.	Natural	Long-shot	25″	Good	Speech	1	Good	No
The flute is a reed instrument. (T-F)	Natural	Medium "	5″	Good "	Speech Sound	1½	Poor	No
The mouthpiece of a double reed woodwind is connected with the main part of the instrument by a ———.	Natural	Close-up	5″	Excellent	Speech and sound "	5½ 7½	Good	Yes
Butterfly eggs are usually laid 1. on the leaves of plants 2. in shallow ponds 3. in nests, built by the adult 4. in a hole in the ground.	Natural	Close-up Medium	18″ 7″	Excellent "	Speech "	2 5	Good	Yes
The woodwind instrument capable of producing the highest notes is the 1. piccolo 2. flute 3. clarinet 4. bassoon.	Natural	Medium	20″	Good	Sound	9	Poor	No

TABLE XXII (*Continued*)

TEST ITEM	TYPE OF PHOTOGRAPHY	FOCAL LENGTH	SCENE LENGTH	QUALITY OF LIGHT	SPEECH OR OTHER SOUND	MINUTE IN PICTURE	INTEGRATION OF SOUND AND SCENE	REPETITION
The only symphony orchestra brass instrument not having valves is the ———.	Natural	Close-up " Medium "		Very good " Good "	Picture alone " " "		Poor	Yes
Three of the following brass instruments have valves. Which *one* does *not* have valves? 1. French horn 2. Trumpet 3. Trombone 4. Tuba.	Natural	Close-up " Medium "		Very good " Good "	Picture alone " " "		Poor	No
The brasses are mostly bass instruments. (T-F)	Natural	Various shots of each			Sound		Poor	No
The tone quality of the oboe is 1. military and dramatic 2. pure and soft 3. penetrating and melancholy 4. noble and sonorous.	Natural	Medium "	15″ 15″	Good "	Speech and sound Speech	3 3½	Poor Poor	No No
Three of the following instruments are used in the symphony orchestra. Which one is *not* used in the symphony orchestra? 1. Mandolin 2. Cello 3. Viola 4. Double bass	(General recall)	questions for observation and			Sound "		Poor	No

Item								
The tones of the French horn are more 1. shrill 2. mellow than those of the trumpet.	Natural	Close-up	Various	Good	Sound "	2 5	Poor	No
The lowest tones of the brass choir are produced by the ———.	Natural	Medium Close-up	40"	Good Excellent	Sound "	9	Poor	Yes
If there were not plant life there could be no animal life. (T-F)	Natural	No related scene	20"		Speech alone		Poor	No
The string choir is the most important group of the symphony orchestra because . . . . (E-C)	Natural	Long shot	30"	Good	Speech alone		Poor	No
The chief difference between the bass drum and tympani is that the bass drum . . . while the tympani . . . . (E-C)	Natural	Medium Close-up	10" 20"	Good "	Speech and sound Sound	4 8	Poor	No
The number of valves usually found on valved brass instruments is ———.	Natural	Close-up " " Medium "		Very good " " Good "	Picture alone " " "	Various	Poor	Yes
The violin is the most useful orchestral instrument because 1. it usually plays soprano parts 2. it has the greatest expressive ability 3. it has more strings than the other stringed instruments 4. it is the easiest to play.	Natural	Medium Close-up	20"	Good Excellent	Speech Sound	3	Poor	No

inherent in the sound picture. This complete integration of sight and sound gives birth to a new art, an art no less exacting in the demand made upon creative effort and interpretative skill than painting, architecture, and music.

The utilization of pictorial and sound composition elements should be guided, in so far as possible, by experimental evidence. The data of the present study suggest lines along which such experimentation might be carried on. In addition, an analysis of these data affords preliminary results which indicate desirable trends in production technique.

METHOD OF ANALYZING COMPOSITION ELEMENTS

An analysis was made of those individual items occurring in both the initial and final tests, the answers to which were furnished either directly or indirectly by the films as well as by the units of instruction. These items, numbering 186,[1] were ranked according to the superiority of experimental pupils over control pupils in the number responding correctly to the test items. Each of these ranked items was then analyzed in terms of the composition elements by which it was presented in the sound picture. The elements used for the high group of test items were compared with the elements used for the low group of items. This technique not only showed the effectiveness of various composition elements over the usual methods of presenting subject matter in the classroom, but also permitted detailed study of the relative effectiveness of specific composition elements.

Those items occurring in the highest and lowest quarters of the distribution were analyzed in terms of the picture composition elements utilized in the presentation of concepts which they measured.[2] This analysis involved a consideration of the following elements: (1) type of photography (whether natural, slow motion, animation, superimposed, composite, or microscopic); (2) focal length (whether close-up, medium, or long shot);

[1] Of these 186 test items, 162 were answered correctly by more pupils of the experimental group than of the control group.

[2] A staff of three professionally qualified individuals assisted the author in making this analysis. This staff was composed of J. A. Brill, Research Associate in Music and Fine Arts, M. A. Brodshaug, Research Associate in Science, and R. F. Chapman, Assistant Director of Production, Erpi Picture Consultants, Inc. Table XXII presents the composite results of these individual judgments. The analysis was made without knowledge of the position of the items within the highest and lowest quarters.

(3) scene length (time of scene in seconds); (4) quality of scene lighting (specific scenes rated on the basis of a five-point scale as follows: excellent, very good, good, fair, and poor); (5) sound, speech, and picture sound; (6) time section of film in which scene occurred (during the minute of the film from the first to the tenth); (7) repetition (including cutback of scenes and repetition of the same ideas with varied scene and speech treatment in one or more instances); and (8) integration of audio-visual elements.

There were 46 test items in each of the highest and lowest 25 per cent of the distribution. Table XXII furnishes examples of individual items with an accompanying analysis of each.

RESULTS OF ANALYSIS OF COMPARATIVE ELEMENTS

Type of Photography

The number of scenes available was not sufficient to furnish evidence as to the superiority of one type of photography over another. The great majority of scenes involved natural photography in both the highest and lowest quarters of the distribution, 68 in the former and 75 in the latter. There was almost an equal amount of animation, slow motion, and time lapse photography in both the highest and lowest sections.

Focal Length of Scenes

Of the sixty-eight separate scenes in the highest quarter of the items, forty-seven were presented by the "close-up," nineteen by the "medium," and two by the "long" focal length. This means that of the concepts presented by these scenes which were measured by the tests, 69 per cent were "close-up," 28 per cent were "medium," and 3 per cent were "long shots."

Of the seventy-five separate scenes in the lowest quarter of the distribution, twenty-five were "close-up," forty-eight were "medium," and two were "long shots." In other words, 33 per cent of the scenes in the lowest quarter were "close-up," 64 per cent were "medium," and 3 per cent were "long shots."

This evidence seems to indicate that the "close-up" is superior to the "medium" or "long shots" in portraying the type of concepts involved in the test items of the present study. In order to become conclusive this interpretation must be subjected to much additional study in the presentation of other types of concepts. Also (and this applies to the other interpretations given in this chapter), a completely thorough study of this element of composition would necessitate a comparison of the effectiveness of scenes presenting identical subject material.

Scene Length

The lengths of the various scenes in the highest quarter of the distribution ranged from seven to one hundred twenty seconds. The median scene length was thirty seconds. This was also the modal point of the highest quarter.

The scene lengths of the lowest quarter of the distribution ranged from six to one hundred fifty seconds. The median length was twenty seconds. This was also the modal point of the lowest distribution. For the presentation of concepts similar to those in the films used in the experiment, it seems that within the limits indicated the longer scene is superior.

Quality of Lighting

The quality of lighting in the films used in this experiment was on the whole very good. In fact, of more than two hundred scenes which were measured by one hundred eighty-six of the test items included in this study, only one was judged to be poor from the standpoint of permitting the average person to determine easily the complete action on the screen.

The quality of lighting of the individual scenes was ranked according to a five-point scale as follows: excellent, very good, good, fair, poor.

The sixty-eight scenes in the highest quarter of the distribution were rated as follows: excellent, 37; very good, 9; good, 18; fair, 4; poor, none. The seventy-five scenes in the lowest quarter of the distribution were rated as follows: excellent, 18; very good, 7; good, 46; fair, 3; poor, 1.

The per cent of items judged to be excellent or very good in the highest quarter was 68 per cent; in the lowest quarter, 33 per cent. Those rated good in the highest quarter were 26 per cent; in the lowest, 61 per cent. Those rated fair in the highest quarter were 6 per cent; in the lowest, 4 per cent. There was none rated poor in the highest quarter and only 1 per cent in the lowest. It will be noted that the proportion of scenes rated excellent or very good in the highest quarter is twice that in the lowest quarter. This is true even though 94 per cent of the scenes of both distributions were ranked "good" or better.

From the results of this analysis it appears that the quality of scene lighting is a highly important element to be considered in producing educational films and that even within the limits of good lighting any added quality will result in a definitely favorable return in clarifying and intensifying the concepts presented.

Speech, Other Sound, and Picture

An examination of Table XXII will reveal the number of concepts which depend upon speech, other sound, or picture alone, or combinations of these elements for their presentation. There are seventy concepts which are measured by the test items in the highest quarter and eighty-six concepts in the lowest.[3] For the purpose of analysis these concepts were classified according to the manner of their presentation as follows: (1) speech and picture, (2) speech, other sound, and picture, (3) sound other than speech, and picture, (4) picture alone, and (5) speech alone. Table XXIII gives the numbers and per cents of these scenes in the highest and lowest quarters of the distribution.

TABLE XXIII

COMPOSITION OF SCENES IN TERMS OF SPEECH, OTHER SOUND, AND PICTURE

METHOD OF PRESENTATION	HIGHEST QUARTER		LOWEST QUARTER	
	No. of Scenes	% of Scenes	No. of Scenes	% of Scenes
Speech and picture	42	60	21	24
Speech, other sound, and picture ...	17	24	16	19
Sound other than speech, and picture	6	9	24	28
Picture alone	5	7	21	24
Speech alone	0	0	4	5
Total	70	100	86	100

It may be noted that of the seventy concepts of the highest quarter, 60 per cent involved speech and picture; 24 per cent speech, other sound, and picture; 9 per cent sound other than speech, and picture; 7 per cent, picture alone; and none was

[3] One film scene may involve two or more concepts.

presented by speech alone. Of the eighty-six concepts of the lowest quarter, 24 per cent involved speech and picture; 19 per cent speech, other sound, and picture; 28 per cent sound other than speech, and picture; 24 per cent picture alone; and 5 per cent were presented by speech alone without other sound or picture.

From these data it appears that the most effective presentation of concepts as measured by the test items of this experiment is made by the use either of speech and picture combined or of speech, other sound, and picture combined. The least effective presentation seems to be the use of sound and picture combined (without accompanying speech) or picture alone (without speech or sound) or speech alone (without picture or sound). This interpretation is supported by the fact that 84 per cent of the concepts in the highest quarter were presented either by speech and picture, or by speech, other sound, and picture; while in the lowest quarter, only 43 per cent of the concepts involved were presented by these methods. However, only 16 per cent of the concepts of the highest quarter were presented by the three methods—sound and picture (without accompanying speech), picture alone (without speech or other sound), and speech alone (without picture or sound)—while in the lowest quarter 57 per cent of the concepts were presented by these three methods. As will be discussed later, it appears that the proper integration of these audio-visual elements requires a judicious selection of one of the two most effective methods, a combination of speech and picture, or a combination of speech, other sound, and picture, depending upon the nature of the concepts to be presented. If extensive repeated research confirms these findings, it would seem that their importance to the future of education can hardly be overestimated.

Section of Film in Which Scene Occurred

A study of the number of scenes occurring in each minute of the films revealed the fact that there was an approximately equal number for each of the highest and lowest quarters. The median for each quarter was the fifth minute of the film. This seems to indicate that the position of a given scene within a one-reel (ten-minute) sound film is unimportant in so far as effective presentation is concerned.

Repetition

A study was made of the concepts upon which the test items were based in the highest and lowest quarters to determine whether or not these concepts were repeated within the film.

In the highest group of items approximately 70 per cent of the concepts were repeated at least once. In the lowest group of items approximately 30 per cent were repeated at least once.

This evidence seems to indicate that repetition is an important element in effective subject matter presentation.

Integration of Audio-Visual Elements

By audio-visual integration is meant the fusion of the audio and visual elements of composition in such a manner as to result in their greatest mutual reinforcement in the most effective presentation of subject matter. For the purpose of this study, the varying degrees of this integration existing in the scenes of the films are ranked according to a three-point scale—excellent, good, and poor.

In judging the degrees of integration of the various combinations of scenes[4] the following general criterion was considered: A scene should utilize the available possibilities in sight and sound so that each serves as an indispensable complement of the other. More specifically, the following questions were asked of each scene: Where sound other than speech was essential to a complete presentation of concept was it used? Was the explanatory speech confined to a simple and concrete presentation or was it burdened with irrelevant or immaterial terminology? Did any sound tend to distract attention from the pertinent and important elements of the scene because of disproportionate and unnatural amplification? Were there any distracting elements of either sight or sound occurring in the scene? Did the speech or other sound tend to direct attention to the important elements of the scene?

Examples of scenes which represent the degrees of integration by which certain scenes of the films were judged are given below.

Example 1. Bees, in visiting flowers, accidentally get pollen on their bodies.

The concept necessary to the proper response is indicated in the

---

[4] Two or more separate scenes may of necessity be combined to present one or more concepts.

test item. The scene utilized the elements of speech and picture. Other sound was not used. It was judged that this element was unnecessary to the presentation of the concept. The insect is shown visiting the flower where the actual deposit of pollen from the flower is made on the body.

The explanatory speech of this combination of scenes is simple and concrete without irrelevant or immaterial terminology. There was no other sound to distract attention from the concept, the mastery of which was later to be tested. There were no distracting pictorial or sound elements. The speech directed attention to the important elements of the scene. The pictorial composition of the combination of scenes was judged to be such that it focalized the important elements. This scene, therefore, was judged to be *excellent*.

Example 2. The chief purpose of the double bass is to reinforce the lowest tones of the harmony.

This scene involved explanatory speech, other sound, and picture. The speech directed attention to the purpose of the double bass. The visual elements made possible an identification of the objects discussed. The other sound in the form of actual music tones completed the presentation of the specific concept. This sound other than speech was essential; the explanatory speech was simple and concrete and included no irrelevant or immaterial terminology. There were no distracting sound elements. There were no distracting pictorial elements. The focalization of the elements of the scene was clear and distinct. This combination of scenes was judged to be *excellent*.

Example 3. Tiger beetles are found where the soil is sandy and dry.

Sound other than speech was not used in this combination of scenes. It was judged to be unnecessary to the mastery of the concept involved. The explanatory speech was simple and concrete. None of the sound distracted attention from the important elements of the scenes. This combination of scenes was judged to be *good*. Although both sandy and dry soil were shown in the scenes, these qualities were not emphasized pictorially. For this reason the integration of the audiovisual elements could not be rated *excellent*.

Example 4. During the playing of the string choir selections, the position of the conductor is ———

This combination of scenes upon which the mastery of this concept depends did not utilize all the elements of sight and sound which might have been utilized by means of the talking picture as a medium of instruction. The sound other than speech which was present in these scenes was unnecessary to a complete presentation of the concept. There was no explanatory speech. Accompanying music was such as to distract attention from the elements of the scene upon which the mastery of this particular concept depended. A complete integration of audio-visual elements of this section of the film would have required explanatory speech in order to present effectively the concept which was measured by this test item. As was pointed out above, this speech was completely lacking. This combination of scenes was, therefore, rated *poor*.

The number and per cent of scenes rated "excellent," "good," and "poor," so far as integration of audio-visual elements is concerned, are indicated in Table XXIV for the highest and lowest quarters.

TABLE XXIV

INTEGRATION OF AUDIO-VISUAL ELEMENTS

QUALITY OF INTEGRATION	HIGHEST QUARTER		LOWEST QUARTER	
	No of Scenes	% of Scenes	No. of Scenes	% of Scenes
Excellent	29	63	6	13
Good	14	30	9	19
Poor	3	7	33	69
Total........................	46	100	48	101

From Table XXIV it can be seen that for the highest quarter of test items there were 46 combinations of scenes, and for the lowest quarter, 48. Of the forty-six combinations of scenes involved in the highest quarter of the distribution, 29 were ranked excellent from the standpoint of integration, 14 good, and 3 poor. In the forty-eight combinations of scenes in the lowest quarter, 6 were ranked excellent, 9 good, and 33 poor. In other words, in 93 per cent of those scenes which resulted in the greatest superiority of experimental over control groups, "excellent" or "good" integration of sight and sound elements was judged to be achieved. On the other hand, in the scenes which resulted in the lowest superiority of experimental over control groups, these degrees of integration were judged to be achieved in only 32 per cent of the cases.

For the seven per cent of the scenes in the highest quarter in which the integration was judged to be "poor," it seems that other desirable elements of composition which were utilized in the production of the scenes must have overcome the effects of poor integration sufficiently to result in a presentation which was distinctly superior to that used in ordinary classroom teaching.

For the thirteen per cent of the scenes in the lowest quarter in which integration was judged to be excellent, it seems that other desirable elements of composition must have been lacking to the extent that the desirable effect of excellent integration was somewhat overcome, as evidenced by the fact that these scenes were among those which resulted in the lowest superiority of experimental over control groups.

It seems, therefore, from this analysis that the integration of audio-visual elements is of maximum importance in the production of educational sound films.

SUMMARY

It may be seen that the production of the educational sound film involves many elements of composition which on the surface are not discernible. The foregoing analysis will indicate that there are many of these elements of picture composition which are highly important. Much has been said about the superiority of the film in which sound other than speech is presented, but from this study there seems to be no direct evidence to prove that such sound is necessary to clarify concepts unless it is used to present concepts directly involving such sound. The most important elements of composition involved in producing an effective educational sound film seem to be, from the data available, the proper integration of audio-visual elements, a generous use of the "close-up" focal length, excellent lighting of scenes, and a judicious use of repetition. It is reasonable to conclude that the sound film, in order to be effective as a teaching medium, must combine into a completely integrated whole all those elements which contribute to effective subject matter presentation.

SUGGESTIONS FOR FURTHER RESEARCH IN SOUND FILM COMPOSITION

A still greater refinement of the procedure suggested in this chapter will necessitate:

1. A complete study of the relationship between the elements of composition used and the relative effectiveness of the presenta-

tion of subject matter presented in the manner suggested by each of the other elements of composition. In order to isolate the effectiveness of each from the influence of the others it would be necessary to utilize the partial correlation technique.

2. A more incisive analysis of the photographic and sound elements in specific composition techniques.

3. A wider range of specific film scenes. Instead of some ninety situations, a complete study would probably involve some five hundred.

4. A more complete analysis of repetition. This is important in order to determine the optimum amount and kind.

5. A consideration of the comparative effectiveness of various elements of film composition at varying age and grade levels.

CHAPTER VII

SUMMARY

THE purpose of the study which has been described in the preceding chapters was twofold:

1. To determine the relative effectiveness (a) of teaching with the aid of certain educational talking pictures in the fields of natural science and music in Grades V and VII, respectively, and (b) of the usual methods of classroom instruction.

2. To make an analysis of the composition elements of certain scenes of the talking pictures used in the experiment to serve as an introduction to the study of the relative effectiveness of these elements of composition.

DESCRIPTION OF EXPERIMENT

The sound pictures used in the experiment were based on units of instruction written by workers trained in the fields of science and music, with due consideration of modern educational theories and practices. The units of instruction served as courses of study for the experimentation. They were: in *natural science*—Butterflies, Beetles, Amphibians, and Growth of Plants; in *music*—The Symphony Orchestra and Its Instruments (the String Choir, the Woodwind Choir, the Brass Choir, and the Percussion Group).

The natural science units were studied in the second half of the fifth grade; the music units, in the second half of the seventh grades of junior high schools. Approximately 950 fifth grade pupils in 32 classes, 1,425 seventh grade pupils in 32 classes, and 64 teachers participated in the experiment. Five cities from three states were chosen: New York City and Schenectady, N. Y., Camden and Elizabeth, N. J., and Baltimore, Md.

The experimental-control technique utilizing the equated teacher method was followed throughout the experiment. The pupils of the control group were taught by the ordinary classroom methods without the aid of talking pictures. The pupils of the experimental group, however, were presented with three showings of each educational talking picture during the course of each unit. Teachers of both groups received units of instruction upon which the pictures were based, which served as courses of study. It may be noted that the control teachers utilized teaching methods with which they were familiar, while the experimental teachers were utilizing talking pictures for the first time.

As an objective check on teacher ability the Jacobs Teacher Efficiency Rating Scale was used. The results of the check indicated that the difference in the average rating of the teachers in the experimental and control groups was negligible.

The Pintner Rapid Survey Intelligence Test, Form B, was administered to all pupils. The results of this test indicate that the natural science groups were well matched on the basis of intelligence. In music, there was a statistically significant difference in average intelligence quotients favoring the control group.

Objective tests, devised to measure the pupils' initial information concerning each of the four units of instruction in natural science and in music, were administered. Each of the initial tests was composed of approximately fifty items which included essay completion, one-word completion, multiple (four) choice, two choice, and true-false types.

The results of the initial tests in natural science indicate that in every test, with the exception of that on Beetles, the average score made by the control group was higher than that made by the experimental group. In only one of these units, Growth of Plants, however, was the difference statistically significant. In music, the initial information of the control group was superior to that of the experimental group in every one of the four units. For three of these units the differences may be considered statistically significant.

The class teaching of the four units of instruction began two weeks after the administration of the intelligence and initial tests. Each unit was taught during a two weeks' period. Both natural science and music groups received 150 minutes of instruction for each unit. The three ten-minute presentations of each talking picture to the experimental groups were part of the 150 minutes of class instruction. The teachers of the control groups were allowed to use any teaching device, except motion pictures, within the time limits set. No teacher was permitted to see any of the tests and no teacher of control classes was allowed to see any of the talking pictures during the experimental period. At the end of each unit of instruction a comprehensive final test based on the material in the unit of instruction and comparable to the initial test was administered.

Four weeks after the completion of the fourth unit of instruction the initial tests were repeated as recall tests. The teachers were not informed, prior to the date set, that recall tests would be administered.

RESULTS OF FINAL TESTS

The final test gains over the initial tests indicate that these talking pictures made distinct contributions to learning. The average gains made by the experimental and control groups in the individual natural science and music units are shown graphically in Chart I. It can be seen that the difference in average gains for the combined cities was greater for the experimental group than for the control group in the case of every unit stud-

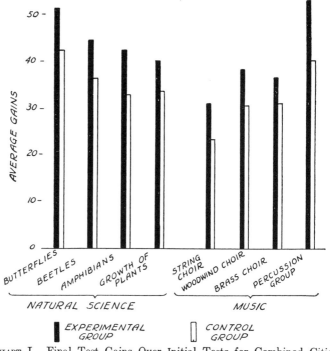

CHART I. Final Test Gains Over Initial Tests for Combined Cities

ied. The critical ratios of the differences between the averages indicate that the superiority of the experimental group was a true superiority in every instance. The per cents of superiority ranged from 22 to 30 in the natural science units and from 18 to 34 in the music units.

The average gain in the total natural science test made by the experimental group was 180 points, and that made by the control group, 143 points. This is a statistically significant difference (critical ratio, 9.55[1]). The per cent of superiority of the experimental group in natural science was 26.

The average gain in the total music test made by the experimental group was 167 points; by the control group, 132 points. This difference is also statistically significant (critical ratio, 9.52[1]). The per cent of superiority of the experimental group in music was 27.

The average gains made on those test items, the answers to which were furnished directly or indirectly by the talking pictures as well as by the units of instruction, indicate specific contributions of these talking pictures. These results are shown graphically in Chart II.

A study of Chart II reveals that there was a marked difference in favor of the experimental group in the case of every unit studied, in both natural science and music, in average gains on the picture-unit items. The per cents of superiority ranged from 41 to 60 in the natural science units and from 20 to 37 in the music units.

On the picture-unit items of the total natural science test for all cities combined, the per cent of superiority of the experimental group was 52. In the case of the total music test the superiority of the experimental group was 31 per cent. The critical ratios were 16.32 and 10.65, respectively, indicating statistically significant differences.

Average gains made by both groups on the non-picture items of the individual tests are shown in Chart III.

In only one of the natural science unit tests (Butterflies) was there a significant difference in average gains favoring the control group. In fact, in one of the unit tests, Amphibians, the difference, though not statistically significant, actually favored the experimental group. For all the natural science tests com-

---

[1] A critical ratio of 3.00 or more indicates statistical significance.

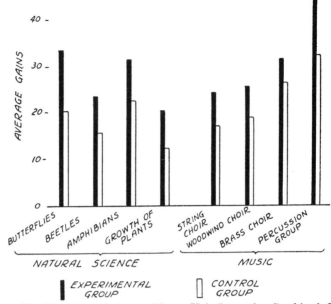

CHART II. Final Test Gains on Picture-Unit Items for Combined Cities

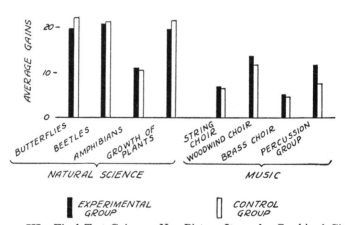

CHART III. Final Test Gains on Non-Picture Items for Combined Cities

bined, the difference between the average gains was but 1 point.

In music the experimental group excelled the control group in average gains on non-picture test items in every unit studied. Test results of two of the units (Woodwind Choir and Percussion

Group) indicate differences that are statistically significant. The per cents of superiority of the experimental group for the four unit tests were: String Choir, 35; Woodwind Choir, 13; Percussion Group, 47, Brass Choir, 3.

This study of averages made on the non-picture items seems to indicate that the marked superiority of the experimental group in average gains made on picture-unit items in natural science and music was produced without sacrificing the subject matter not presented specifically by the talking pictures.

EFFECTIVENESS OF THE TALKING PICTURES IN GROUPS OF BELOW AVERAGE AND ABOVE AVERAGE INTELLIGENCE LEVELS

The final test gains made in the total natural science and music tests for groups of below average and above average intelligence levels in the combined cities are shown graphically in Chart IV.

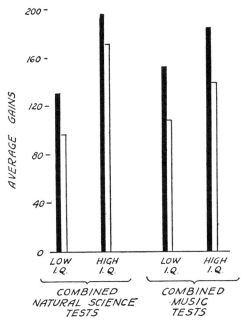

CHART IV. Final Test Gains Over Initial Tests for Groups of Below and Above Average Intelligence Levels for Combined Cities

The average gains made by the experimental groups in natural science and music exceeded those made by the control groups by statistically significant amounts in both low and high levels. It appears, therefore, that the talking pictures make distinct contributions to the learning of pupils of below and above average intelligence levels.

RESULTS OF RECALL TESTS

The recall test gains made over the initial tests are shown in Chart V.

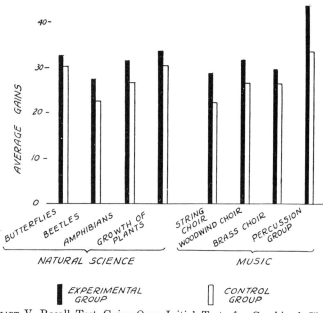

CHART V. Recall Test Gains Over Initial Tests for Combined Cities

From Chart V it can be seen that the average recall test gains over the initial test were greater for the experimental group in every unit of study. In natural science the per cents of superiority ranged from 9 to 18; in music, from 14 to 32.

The experimental groups exceeded the control groups in the total natural science and music recall test gains for all cities combined. These differences are statistically significant. The superiority of the experimental groups was 26 per cent in natural science and 22 per cent in music.

Comparison of the experimental and control groups in regard to the per cents of the final tests retained, as measured by the recall tests, is presented graphically in Chart VI.

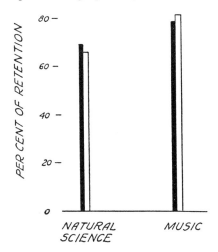

EXPERIMENTAL GROUP   CONTROL GROUP

CHART VI. Percentage of Retention of Total Final Test as Measured by Total Recall Test for Combined Cities

Chart VI shows that the per cent of retention of final test information is greater for the experimental group in the case of the total natural science test and greater for the control group in the total music test. Neither of the differences, however, represents statistical certainty.

It appears from the evidence furnished by the recall test results that the talking pictures used in this experiment made a lasting contribution to learning in natural science and music.

EFFECTIVENESS OF SPECIFIC ELEMENTS OF TALKING PICTURE COMPOSITION OF THE FILMS USED IN THE EXPERIMENT

A study was made of the effectiveness of the elements of composition of certain scenes from the films used in the experiment as measured by the comparative test gains of the experimental and control groups. This study seems to indicate that those elements of composition which are of greatest importance in the production of the educational talking picture are the proper integration of audio-visual elements, a generous use of the "close-up" focal length, excellent lighting of scenes, and a judicious use of repetition.

SUMMARY

Chart VII presents graphically the comparisons between the gains made by the experimental and control groups on final test

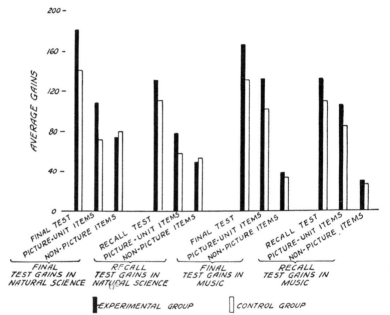

CHART VII. Total Science and Music Gains Over Initial Test for Combined Cities

gains, gains on picture-unit items, gains on non-picture items, recall test gains, recall gains on picture-unit items, and recall gains on non-picture items.

In summary, it appears that the talking pictures used in this experiment made marked and lasting contributions to learning, both in the natural science units and in the music units. These contributions, however, were made without the loss of learning other elements of subject matter of the units not included in the talking pictures themselves.

CHAPTER VIII

PROBLEMS FOR FUTURE RESEARCH

THE present study indicates the effectiveness of the educational sound picture as an aid to the teaching of certain units of instruction in natural science and music. This demonstration of effectiveness within these rather narrow ranges of instruction suggests many other possibilities for fruitful research, the results of which should be of greatest importance to the whole field of education. Some of these areas of research which seem most promising are discussed in this chapter.

EXTENSION OF RANGE OF PRESENT CURRICULUM

There are certain human limitations to learning which have seriously restricted the development of the curriculum in all levels of education. Some of these are: the difficulty with which the individual acquires concepts which depend almost wholly upon verbalism for their presentation; his inability to perceive certain movements in nature because of the rapidity or slowness with which they occur; his inability to see objects which, because of their extremely small size or because of their great distance in space, are beyond the range of the unaided human eye; his inability to hear sounds which, because of their extremely small volume or because of their great distance from the hearer, are beyond the limits of unaided reception; and his inability to reach backward into the past and reproduce objects and actions which contribute to the conditioning of his present environment.

These rather obvious limitations have to some extent been overcome by mechanical means which have been developed in the course of scientific research during the nineteenth and twentieth centuries. The modern telescope has enabled the individual to make excursions into space which until recently were impossible. The microscope has brought into the range of human vision objects which, without its assistance, would have been forever beyond his perception. The moving picture camera has

89

extended the arm of the interpretative artist so that for a good many years he has been able to record for the eyes of the future, objects in action which hitherto have passed into unreality to be reproduced only by means of indefinite forms of verbalism. The slow motion and time lapse devices which have been added to this instrument have contributed to the clarification of many concepts which in the past were beyond the perception of the individual learner. Modern sound recording, amplifying, and transmitting devices have made many significant and fundamental contributions upon which the reality of concepts depends.

Although these products of modern invention have been available, some of them for many years, education has, to a great degree, continued to depend largely upon the printed word for the transfer of ideas. This dependence upon the product of the printing press has resulted in many restrictions in the scope and range of the curriculum. The aims and objectives of education have been established sometimes with, and often without, a conscious realization of these restrictions imposed by this mechanical invention. A glance into the activities of the traditional primary school will reveal the nature of these restrictions. At the time of his entrance into the school, the normal pupil has during the first five or six years of his life already attained a rather profound mastery of several tools of learning in the form of the five senses. Through the use of these tools, learning from his immediate environment has proceeded at a very rapid rate. By the time he starts to school, however, the returns from his immediate environment have begun to diminish. In order for full development to continue, a significant elaboration of this environment must be furnished. This elaboration of environment is one of the responsibilities which the school must assume. It is generally true that this institution is so organized that it is literally forced to await the mastery of additional tools of learning before it can proceed at a very rapid rate toward the fulfillment of this responsibility. It is needless to recall the emphasis which at present is placed upon these "tool subjects" of the traditional elementary school curriculum. By far the most important of these is reading. Many concepts which are fundamental to the future elaboration of the pupil's environment he cannot acquire with the optimum degree of mastery through the use of this "tool" because of the complexity of certain mental processes which learning through reading presupposes.

The sound picture has at its disposal, in numerous desirable combinations, the inherent advantages of the telescope, the microscope, the moving picture camera (with its many devices such as slow motion, time lapse photography, and animation), and sound recording and amplifying devices. Clarification of concepts through this medium is not necessarily dependent upon the "tool subjects" of the curriculum. Thus, the sound picture holds out to those responsible for the construction of the curriculum a unique challenge.

This challenge can be met by the application of instruments of research, many of which are now available, some of which have yet to be developed. What effect, if any, will the use of these mechanical devices have upon the mastery of the time-honored "tool subjects" of the present curriculum? Are there objectives of education which are withheld until the later years of school life solely because of this dependence upon the mastery of concepts which are too "difficult" to present through reading? Can certain objectives be attained with the aid of these products of modern invention? Can much time of the school be saved and energy of teachers conserved for more important duties?

It is possible that the answers to these questions would release the curriculum specialist from many of the restrictive influences which are inherent in the present methods of subject matter presentation, to the end that the extension of the curriculum would be determined not by the present limitations to learning, but by the needs of the race.

SELECTION OF METHODS OF SUBJECT-MATTER PRESENTATION

From the results of extended research it should be possible, from any given area of instruction to classify the elements of subject matter involved according to the optimum method of their effective and economical presentation in some such categories as the following:

1. Subject matter which can be presented best by means of the printed word.

2. Subject matter which can be presented best by the lecture method.

3. Subject matter which can be presented best by the laboratory method.

4. Subject matter which can be presented best through group discussion.

5. Subject matter which can be presented best by mechanical mediums.

By effective and economical presentation is meant that presentation which is effective from the standpoint of clarifying concepts and economical in terms of time and energy required of pupils, teachers, or both, to accomplish desired objectives.

The producer of educational talking pictures should obviously be concerned primarily with those elements of subject matter which can best be presented through mechanical mediums. It can be seen that these elements cannot be determined without a broad grasp of the problems involved in all the other types of subject matter presentation. This indicates, then, a need for the development of a field of research unique in the history of education—the analysis of subject matter in terms of objectives and optimum methods of presentation.

REFINEMENT OF TESTING

The student of the effects of sound pictures must recognize the limitations of testing devices now prevalent. He cannot, however, be content merely to point out the shortcomings of these devices. He must endeavor to supplement present testing devices in order to measure results which come from participation of children in situations that are more nearly real life situations than those presented by ordinary instructional devices.

The appraisal of sound pictures involves a consideration of the more dynamic aspects of learning. By means of the talking picture the learner experiences life unfolding, not through the medium of inadequate symbols of the printed page, but with all the detail and fullness of the real situation. Does this medium develop appreciations and attitudes which are fundamental to an adequate integration of the learner with his total environment? How can such appreciations and attitudes be measured by objective methods? How can the amount and kind of stimulus which such a medium offers toward new and further learning be determined?

It is only through the development of adequate tests that the scope and value of an instructional medium which does not acknowledge the common limitations of the unaided human senses can be more completely determined.

OTHER PROBLEMS FOR RESEARCH

Some of the other specific problems for research in the field of educational sound pictures follow:

Investigation of the effectiveness of the talking picture in teaching very large groups.

This would involve a study of the types and amounts of subject materials of the curriculum which can be presented to many groups brought together at one time. It is possible that certain portions of many courses may be presented by the talking picture, thus relieving the teacher of much instruction which can be administered in a routine manner so that his time may be more profitably spent in administering to the individual needs of learners.

Exhaustive study of the effectiveness of specific elements of sound film composition.

This should lead to a continuing improvement of this medium as a teaching vehicle.

Adaptability of the medium in supplementing typical forms and methods of teaching.

Wherein do certain forms of school organizations and specific types of teaching method fail to meet the requirements of sound educational practice? How might the talking picture be made to provide instructional materials which will overcome certain of these shortcomings of typical forms and methods?

Studies in utilization.

Should certain types of talking pictures be shown once or twice and others even more often? What are the optimum procedures to be followed in administering the talking picture on the various levels of education?

Psychological studies with reference to interest at various age and grade levels.

There is need for objective measurement of the relative effectiveness of presentation by talking pictures of instructional materials which previous research has indicated are of general interest at various age and grade levels and those instructional materials which are foreign to the previous experiences of learners at these levels.

Investigation of the effectiveness of the talking picture when used with very small class groups in which self-administering devices are utilized.

This type of activity may suggest the further possibility of increasing in an effective and economical manner the scope of the curriculum of the modern school.

The talking picture in adult education.

The opportunities for the use of this medium in adult education should be thoroughly investigated. Special attention should be given to the effectiveness of the talking picture when utilized to supplement other types of teaching and when used alone to present the complete instructional unit.

These problems for research will depend for their solution upon the coördination and integration of the work of the philosopher, the sociologist, the psychologist, the student of method, the subject matter specialist, the educational administrator, and the expert sound film technician. It will be through this coördination of effort that the educational talking picture will assume its proper position of usefulness in the field of education.

BIBLIOGRAPHY

BRILL, JAMES A. *Teacher's Handbook—The Symphony Orchestra and Its Instruments.* New York City: Electrical Research Products, Inc., 1931. Pp. 36.

BRODSHAUG, MELVIN. *Teacher's Handbook—Amphibians.* New York City: Electrical Research Products, Inc., 1931. Pp. 18.

BRODSHAUG, MELVIN. *Teacher's Handbook—Beetles.* New York City: Electrical Research Products, Inc., 1931. Pp. 25.

BRODSHAUG, MELVIN. *Teacher's Handbook—Butterflies.* New York City: Electrical Research Products, Inc., 1931. Pp. 22.

BRODSHAUG, MELVIN. *Teacher's Handbook—Growth of Plants.* New York City: Electrical Research Products, Inc., 1931. Pp. 20.

CLARK, C. C. *Sound Motion Pictures as an Aid in Classroom Teaching.* New York University School of Commerce, Accounts and Finances, Unpublished Ph.D. Thesis.

EADS, LAURA KRIEGER AND STOVER, EDGAR M. *Talking Pictures in Teacher Training.* New York City: Erpi Picture Consultants, Inc., Unpublished.

Erpi Picture Consultants, Inc. *A Handbook of Standards for Educational Talking Pictures.* 250 West 57th Street, New York City, 1932. Pp. 23.

Sound Films in Schools. Fleet Street, London, England: "The Schoolmaster" Publishing Company, 1931. Pp. 120.

Sound Motion Pictures as a Factor in Education. New York City: Fox Film Corporation, 1931. Pp. 11.

APPENDIX

APPENDIX A

TYPICAL UNIT OF INSTRUCTION

TEACHER'S HANDBOOK FOR THE UNIT AMPHIBIAN*

I. *General Objective:*

To study the characteristics, habits, and life cycles of amphibia.

II. *Specific Objectives:*

1. To learn the life history of the frog, of the toad, and of the salamander.
2. To discover the characteristics and the habits of the different amphibia.
3. To become acquainted with the pond as the home of interesting and varied forms of life.
4. To appreciate the usefulness of the frog and the toad.
5. To develop the habit of accurate observation in this field.
6. To learn to regard the animals of this group without superstition or fear.

III. *Overview:*

Amphibians include toads, frogs, and salamanders. This group is interesting in that it represents what is probably a survival stage of development, midway between water animals and land animals. The amphibians, named from two Greek words meaning double life, are so called because the first stage of growth takes place in water and the second stage on land.

The first stage is marked by developments characteristic of the fish group. Amphibians are hatched from eggs and while young resemble very closely certain kinds of fish.

The second stage is marked by radical changes in body structure, which permit adaptation to an entirely different environment. These changes require from two weeks to about two years, depending on the species of amphibia.

There are countless varieties of amphibians ranging from certain tiny toads to such large creatures as the bull-frog, the mud-puppy, and the giant salamander of Japan.

Certain amphibia are of decided economic importance. Toads, and to some extent frogs, assist the gardener and farmer by devouring insects. Frogs' legs are considered quite a delicacy. However, it seems poor economy to destroy such important helpers of man.

* This handbook represents the type of supplementary material which served to guide the teaching of all the units of the experiment both in the control and experimental groups.

IV. *Suggested Activities:*

Several short projects based on the study of amphibia are given below. It is highly desirable that the activity be the result of pupil interest rather than teacher-imposed work. However, when economy of time is necessary, the teacher may set the stage for the unit. Any one or any combination of the following suggestions may be used as the teacher sees fit. At least one of the first three would seem necessary in order to attain the objectives listed. The last three suggestions are more appropriate to the lower grades than the upper.

1. *Aquarium of toad-eggs or tadpoles:* The toad offers the best subject for class observation because of its rapid development and growth. An aquarium may be made by filling a large glass jar with material found at the bottom of the pond, such as sand, rocks, and plant growth. Care should be taken to disturb these substances as little as possible. When the aquarium is ready, it may be stocked with the eggs or tadpoles usually found in the pond in the spring or early summer. The water should be changed regularly, using pond water only.

If possible, it would be well to observe the development of the egg through a microscope or a magnifying glass. As the tadpoles develop they should be fed scum from the pond, green algae, lettuce, fish food, boiled corn meal, pulp of tulip leaves, or hard-boiled eggs. The fishlike character of the tadpoles or polliwogs, as evidence in the tail and gills, should be noted. The development of the hind legs, forelegs, and mouth, and the disappearance of the gills and the tail are interesting stages of growth. The pupils should also watch closely the color changes that take place as the tadpole becomes a real toad.

The fertilization of the egg and the comparison with similar processes in plants are also topics which may be developed in connection with this project.

2. *Cage for frogs and toads:* A cage for adult amphibians can easily be made from a box containing a dish of water, loose dirt, and some grass. Frogs are readily found near ponds in summer and toads are usually very much in evidence following a prolonged rain. At other times toads may be found in moist, dark places under boards and logs. A salamander would also be desirable for the aquarium if the pupils are successful in locating a specimen. They will most probably be found under rocks in the bed of a brook or under logs in damp ravines.

In caring for the specimens the pupils will observe their habits. As the toad snaps up live insects, the pupils can watch the play of its front-hinged tongue. They will be interested to see how the toad drinks, as it simply immerses itself in water and permits the water to soak in through its skin. The toad and the frog may be studied and compared in respect to color, habits, length of jump, method and speed in swimming, action when frightened, food habits, characteristic sounds, breathing movements, temperature of the body, texture of the skin, slime, protective coloration, eyes, ears, nostrils, mouth, teeth, feet, bony structure, and eggs.

The pupils should be required to tend their specimens carefully. After the project has been finished, it would be well to have a ceremony when the frogs or toads are liberated in a safe place out-of-doors. This will impress the pupils with their obligation to protect harmless creatures.

3. *Visit to a pond:* Another project rich in learning activities is a visit to a nearby pond, if the season is suitable. To conserve class time, the teacher should make certain beforehand that the pond contains frogs, tadpoles, or eggs. Before making the trip, it will be wise for the class to discuss methods of securing specimens and important facts to be noted. In this way the pupils can prepare the needed equipment.

To observe the frogs in their habitat, it will be necessary for the pupils to be very quiet and to wait for some time. The pupils should be cautioned that noise will send the frogs under cover. If the trip is made in the spring, pupils may be able to wade in the pond and secure eggs and tadpoles with a fine mesh net.

If time permits, this project may be undertaken as preliminary to the classroom project previously described. The trip to the pond may also take place as part of a general nature-study expedition in the spring, when birds, trees, flowers, and pond life are all observed.

4. *Bulletin board project:* The pupils may collect for the bulletin board a variety of materials dealing with amphibia. This display may include pictures, stories, poems copied from books, and verse which they themselves have created. A daily record of the care of the aquarium and the activities of their specimens is also suitable. Sketches of the life cycle of the frog or the toad, and outline charts of the tadpole's development should prove especially interesting.

5. *Scrapbook:* The preceding project is a class or group activity; this is a project for the individual pupil. Each child may collect and place in a scrapbook materials of the type listed above. The scrapbook has an added value in that it contains, as a permanent record for the pupil, interesting information and poetry which he has gathered in connection with amphibia.

6. *Dramatization:* Since dramatization is a natural activity with children, the writing and acting of short plays dealing with frogs or toads offer stimulating opportunities for correlation with reading, language work, nature study, and expression.

V. *Content:*

1. The Amphibian Group.
2. Tadpoles or Polliwogs.
3. Frogs:
    a. The leopard frog.
    b. The bullfrog.
    c. The green frog.
    d. The wood frog.
    e. The spring peeper.
4. Toads:
5. Salamanders:
    a. The mud-puppy.
    b. The newt and eft.

 c. The spotted salamander.
 d. The two-lined salamander.
 e. The dusky salamander.
 f. The red-backed salamander.

THE AMPHIBIAN GROUP

 The amphibian group constitutes one of the five classes of vertebrate animals. The other classes are mammals, birds, reptiles, and fish. It is somewhat difficult to distinguish some amphibians from certain reptiles. However, it should be remembered that reptiles, in contrast to amphibians, always have scales.

 The word amphibia is of Greek derivation and means "double life." Its use here is explained by the fact that these creatures spend the first part of their lives in water, and the latter part principally on land. In the first stage they possess the characteristics of fish; in the second stage, the characteristics of land animals. It is generally assumed that the amphibians represent a survival stage in the development of water animals into land animals. All amphibia are cold-blooded, which means that they assume the temperature of their environment. It is interesting to note that fish and reptiles are also cold-blooded.

TADPOLES OR POLLIWOGS

 Tadpole is a name applied to most amphibians in one stage of their life cycle. The frog-tadpoles develop from eggs which are generally laid in stagnant water, by the mother frog. They usually hatch in from two to fifteen days, depending on the species and the temperature.

 The young tadpoles resemble catfish or bullheads except that they do not have fins. They have long flat tails which, when swished from side to side, enable them to swim. They breathe through gills on the sides of their bodies. The young tadpole has no mouth; in place of a mouth it has two tiny suckers which exude a sticky substance to enable the tadpole to cling to weeds. Later the mouth develops. The food consists of plant matter, such as green algae, water-weeds, and scum. The traditional enemies of the tadpole are fish, snakes, and water-beetles.

 After a few days tadpoles gradually begin to develop the characteristics of land animals. A membrane grows over the gills, but they are still used for breathing. As water flows in through the nostrils and back over the gills, delicate blood vessels absorb the oxygen of the air dissolved in the water. The water passes through the gills and out of a small opening in the side of the body. Lungs are now developing and after a while the hole in the side closes up. Since frogs and toads have no ribs, they must swallow air and then force it out. This accounts for the pulsation of the membrane under the mouth. The heart, which formerly had only the two chambers characteristic of the fish group, now develops a third chamber. After the hind legs have developed the front legs bud and grow to full proportions. The maturing tadpole begins to acquire a lighter color in place of the nearly black color of the young polliwog. Finally the tail is absorbed. During this process the tadpole does not eat. The tail does not drop off, as is commonly supposed. Toad tadpoles develop into toads in one or two months, while a bullfrog remains in the tadpole stage for two years.

Our tadpole is now a frog or a toad, and some rainy day he will leave the water. The toad never returns except to lay eggs, but most frogs are seldom seen far from the water. The great number of toads seen after a heavy rain formerly made people think that they "rained down"; this, of course, is merely superstition.

FROGS

Frogs vary in color according to species, although most of them are a mottled green and brown, and this enables them to blend well with their environment. This characteristic in animals, so important as a defense, is known as protective coloration. Frogs can still further adapt themselves to their environment by changing color in a very few minutes. Bright colors are prominent during the mating season. The skin is smooth and slippery in texture.

The hind legs, long and powerful, are especially adapted for leaping. The forelegs are short. The toes on the hind legs are webbed to facilitate swimming.

Frogs have a keen sense of smell and of hearing. Although their eyes protrude, they can be drawn in for protection. There is also a membrane which moves up from the lower lid for additional protection. Frogs can absorb water through their skin or obtain it from leaves by means of special glands.

The habits of frogs are interesting. They are carnivorous, since they feed on live insects, snails, or worms. Live insects are caught by thrusting out the tongue, which is fastened in the front of the mouth and curls around the prospective meal. There are teeth in the frog's upper jaw which aid in devouring food.

In the fall frogs begin to hibernate by digging deep into the mud at the bottom of ponds or streams. Breathing now stops and the heart action is very faint. In the spring they again emerge. At night the male frogs can be heard giving their characteristic croak or song. This sound is distinctly a mating call.

Eggs are laid in the spring months from March to June, according to the climate. They are found in clusters in stagnant water, each egg surrounded by a gelatinous mass. The female deposits her eggs in the water and they are fertilized by male cells or spermatozoa as they are laid. Some kinds of frogs lay as many as twenty thousand eggs each year, while other kinds seldom lay over a thousand.

Needless to say, most of the eggs never reach the adult frog stage. Just as frogs eat other smaller forms of life, they in turn must beware lest they are eaten by larger animals. They must also be on guard against thoughtless people who want them only for sport. It is important that frogs should be protected since they are not only harmless but are destroyers of insect life.

Leopard frog: The bodies of these frogs measure about four inches in length, with hind legs six inches long. They are commonly found in most parts of North America. Their favorite habitat is in meadows. In color they are gray, brown, or green, but nearly white underneath. A female may lay as many as four thousand eggs. Tadpoles hatch in about two weeks, and at the end of twelve weeks they are three and one-third inches in length. The young frogs are about an inch in length and require three years to mature.

Bullfrog: Some bullfrogs attain a length of seven to eight inches. They are quite common in all parts of the United States and Canada east of the Rockies. They are always found in or very near water. In early summer the female bullfrog lays her eggs, sometimes as many as twenty thousand, on the surface of the pond. Under favorable conditions, the eggs hatch in less than a week. The tadpoles grow to be about six inches long and remain in that stage for two years. This species of frog is green and brown with a cream-colored belly. The familiar "jug-o-rum" is the characteristic call of the bullfrog.

Green frog: This frog, sometimes called "spring frog," is very similar to the bullfrog except that it is much smaller, measuring about four inches in length. Its note is like the twanging of the string of a musical instrument. Its native habitat is in the eastern section of North America.

Wood frog: Wood frogs have the least desire for water of any of our frogs and are generally found in the woods, as the name implies. They average about two inches in length with legs three to four inches long. Their croak has no musical quality. The protective coloration they exhibit is quite interesting, as their color may be changed very easily. There is a dark spot back of their eyes and the lower portions of their bodies are pinkish in color.

Spring peeper: Peepers, common in eastern North America, average one inch in length, with the hind legs two inches long. In color they vary from yellow to a dark brown with darker lines on the body and between the eyes. The female lays her eggs singly among water plants, sometimes as many as eight hundred. They hatch in about twelve days and remain in the tadpole stage from two to three months.

TOADS

Toads are quite similar to frogs in features and habits. Protective coloration is established by their grayish color, hardly distinguishable from the soil. Their dry and warty skin increases their resemblance to the environment. The fluid secreted by the skin, although highly irritating to animals who try to eat toads, will not cause warts on human beings, as many people suppose.

Since the hind legs are not so long and powerful as those of frogs and since the body is more sturdy, one would not expect the toad to be quite so active as the frog. The toad's tongue has a sticky substance which helps it to catch insects, but it has no teeth. Its diet consists of flies, ants, grubs, caterpillars, and other insects. The toad will eat only moving life.

The habits of toads are curious. They are nocturnal, that is, they feed at night. Except when it rains, toads remain hidden in dark and damp places during the day. It is interesting to note that they shed their skin regularly. It splits in three places, then it is drawn into their mouth and swallowed. They hibernate in sand or humus, or in other protected places, during the winter. Forty years is not an unusual age for a toad.

In the spring, they seek water in which to lay their eggs. The eggs are placed usually in two strings, each several feet long.

The toad has many enemies. Ducks, crows, hawks, owls, and snakes seem to find the toad good food. It is often the target for malicious mischief on the part of thoughtless persons.

Of all wild life the toad deserves as much protection as any animal, since it is so useful to the farmer in destroying insects. It is variously estimated that each toad in the garden is worth from five to fifty dollars.

There are several kinds of toads. The common or American toad is about three inches long and shades from light brown to gray in color. The male's call is in the nature of a musical trill. The more important kinds found in the eastern part of the United States are the common toad and Fowler's toad.

SALAMANDERS

Salamanders are often improperly called lizards. Though they look very much like salamanders, lizards are reptiles and have scales. The eggs of lizards do not hatch into tadpoles, but directly into lizards. The salamander's body is slender with a very long tail. All four legs are of the same size and are poorly developed. Its favorite abode is in dark damp places, such as moist cellars, damp wood, and old wells. Because its diet consists mainly of insects, it is of economic value.

Its eggs, laid in water, develop into tadpoles the same as frog and toad eggs. A few kinds of salamanders always remain in the water and retain their gills. Some lay their eggs in sand, and these develop immediately into small salamanders without passing through the tadpole stage.

Salamanders, curiously enough, were thought by people in ancient times to be "fireproof." This, of course, was only a superstition. From that belief, however, the name salamander came to be used for a certain kind of cooking vessel.

Mud-puppy: This salamander is generally about two feet in length. It usually lives in water, where it is very destructive to fish eggs.

Newt and eft: These are about four inches long with slender bodies, colored olive green on the back and yellowish on the under side. They eat insects and are therefore of some economic value, but in one stage of their development they are destructive to fish eggs.

Spotted salamander: This kind is from six to seven inches long. It is black and has yellow spots. It destroys insects, snails, and slugs. Damp cellars are a common habitat.

Two-lined salamander: The two-lined salamander is named from the two lines, one on either side of the body. It is about three inches in length and is yellow in color.

Dusky salamander: The dusky salamander has a thick-set body and is about four inches in length. If the tail is lost, it will be regenerated or replaced in a short time.

Red-backed salamander: This salamander is about four inches long. It is found in eastern North America in woods under logs and stumps.

VI. *Outcomes:*

The objectives of this unit have been achieved if the pupils have attained:

1. A desire to protect frogs and toads.
2. Ability to distinguish between toads and frogs.
3. A fearless attitude toward the amphibia.
4. Knowledge that toads are of great value to the farmer.
5. An understanding of the life cycle of amphibians.
6. Concomitants of accurate observation, joy in discovery, and kindness towards harmless, helpless animals.
7. A deeper interest in the study of nature.

BIBLIOGRAPHY

A. REFERENCES FOR THE TEACHER

1. BASKETT, JAMES N., and DITMARS, R. L.   *The Story of Amphibians.* New York: D. Appleton & Co., 1902.
2. *The Classroom Teacher,* "Reptiles and Amphibians," Vol. 9, pp. 446-466. Chicago: The Classroom Teacher, Inc., 1929.
3. COMSTOCK, A. B.   *Handbook of Nature Study,* Chap. III.   Ithaca: Comstock Publishing Company, 1929.
4. DICKERSON, MARY C.   *Frog Book.*   Garden City: Doubleday, Doran & Co., 1906.
5. HODGE, C. F.   *Nature Study and Life,* pp. 274-284, 478-490.   Boston: Ginn & Co., 1902.
6. HOLTZ, F. L.   *Nature Study,* pp. 148-164.   New York: Charles Scribner's sons, 1908.
7. HORNADAY, WILLIAM T.   *American Natural History,* "Amphibians," pp. 359-371.   New York: Charles Scribner's Sons, 1927.
8. UNITED STATES BUREAU OF FISHERIES.   "Frogs," *Document* 888.
9. UNITED STATES DEPARTMENT OF AGRICULTURE.   "Usefulness of the American Toad," *Farmers' Bulletin* 196.

B. REFERENCES FOR THE PUPIL

1. *The Book of Knowledge,* "The Wonderful Amphibians," Vol. 15, pp. 5453-5458.   New York: Grolier Society, 1929.
2. *Book of Popular Science,* "Water-Born Land Animals," Vol. 12, pp. 4201-4210.   New York: Grolier Society, 1924.
3. Compton's Pictured Encyclopedia, "Frogs and Polliwogs," Vol. 3, pp. 1373-1375.   "Toad," Vol. 8, pp. 3506-3507.   Chicago: F. E. Compton & Co., 1928.
4. DOWNING, E. R.   *Our Living World,* pp. 42-52.   New York: Longmans, Green & Co., 1924.

5. Du Puy, W. A. *Our Animal Friends and Foes,* pp. 9-14. Philadelphia: John C. Winston Co., 1925.

6. *New Human Interest Library,* "The Amphibians," Vol. 2, pp. 203-207. Chicago: The Midland Press, 1928.

7. *New Students' Reference Book,* "Frog," Vol. 2, pp. 719-720; "Toad," Vol. 6, pp. 1917-1918. Cleveland: The S. L. Weedon Company, 1928.

8. Nida, William L., and Stella H. *Science Readers,* Book IV, Chap. 29. Boston: D. C. Heath & Co., 1926.

9. Patch, Edith Marion. *Holiday Pond.* New York: The Macmillan Company, 1929.

10. Patterson, Alice Jean. *Nature Study and Health Education,* Book VI, Chaps. 37, 38 and 39. Normal, Illinois: McKnight and McKnight, 1927.

11. Persing, Ellis C. and Thiele, C. Louis. *Elementary Science by Grades,* Book V, Chap. 4. New York: D. Appleton & Co., 1930.

12. Pierson, C. D. *Among the Pond People.* New York: E. P. Dutton & Co., 1901.

13. *The World Book,* "Frog," Vol. 5, pp. 2625-2626; "Tadpole," Vol. 11, p. 6997, "Toad," Vol. 11, pp. 7189-7193. Chicago: W. F. Quarrie & Co., 1928.

APPENDIX B

TYPICAL SOUND PICTURE CONTINUITY

PERCUSSION GROUP*

SYMPHONY ORCHESTRA SERIES

(Sound Picture Continuity)

(Note: During the showing of the title a selection is being played on the chimes, accompanied by an off-stage orchestra.)

PICTURE ELEMENTS	SOUND OR SPEECH

Scene 1

Foreground. Performer playing.   Selection—"The Chimes."

Scene 2

Semi-close-up: Of performer as he finishes selection.

Scene 3

Full scene. A curtain stage set with percussion instruments. Lecturer and three performers in evening dress are discovered.

The selection you have just heard was played on the chimes, one of the percussion group of the symphony orchestra, a group so named because its instruments must be struck to produce tone.

Scene 4

Semi-close-up: Of lecturer.

One of the most common forms of percussions we find in the bells, an instrument producing chromatic tones.

Scene 5

Medium shot: Of performer playing, followed by medium shots from right and left, showing technique.

Selection—"Silent Night."

* This continuity of the sound picture, Percussion Group, illustrates the type of films used in the experiment.

Scene 6

Panorama shot, medium shot. Performer walks into semi-close-up as he reaches xylophone.

Now the xylophone, although similar to the bells, has wooden bars instead of metal.

Scene 7

Close-up of resonators.

These bars have resonators which enrich the tone. The xylophone is most often used in popular orchestras and as a solo instrument.

Scene 8

Medium: Of performer. Performer plays.

Selection—"Old Folks at Home."

Scene 9

Semi-close-up: Showing hands operating four hammers, then two.

Scene 10

Pan shot: As performer goes to celesta.

The celesta, which is an adaptation of the bells, is one of the most recent inventions in orchestral instruments.

Scene 11

Medium shot of performer at celesta.

The celesta has a greater range than the bells and the performer uses a keyboard instead of striking the bars directly. (Demonstrates by striking arpeggios.)

Scene 12

Close-up: Of resonators.

The celesta also has resonators.

Scene 13

Medium shot over player's shoulder, showing hands, operating keyboard. Performer plays.

Selection—"Last Rose of Summer."

Scene 14

Semi-close-up: Of lecturer.

The drum was probably man's first musical instrument, and the tom-tom is one of its earliest forms.

Scene 15

Close-up: Of tom-tom.

The tom-tom, therefore, is used in primitive rhythms.

Scene 16

Medium shot: Demonstration of tom-tom.

Selection—"Indian Theme."

Scene 17

Pan to bass drum—Demonstration of bass drum.

From this crude beginning have come our modern drums—the bass drum which has the principal rhythmic accent (selection—Introduction "March Militaire")—

Scene 18

Medium: Pan to snare drum. Demonstration of snare drum.

and the snare drum, which often marks the afterbeat. (Same selection repeated)

Scene 19

Medium: Pan to tympani.

The percussion instruments most necessary to a symphony orchestra are the tympani or kettle drums made of copper. The tympani originated in Turkey.

Scene 20

Close-up: Of tympani (indicates pitch by striking each).

Each one has a definite pitch, and is tuned to the composition.

Scene 21

Medium: Of performer playing, from two successive angles.

Selection—"Coronation March"— Meyerbeer.

Scene 22

Medium: Of performer with cut-in short close-up showing pedal action.

When necessary the tympani may be retuned during the playing of a number, either by the handles—or by pedals, which are a recent development.

Scene 23

Foreground, same performer picks up castanets.

The castanets are of Moorish origin. They were adopted by the Spanish after the Moorish invasion during the eleventh century.

Scene 24

Semi-close-up.

Performer clicks castanets to short Spanish melody.

Scene 25

Medium pan across stage to performer holding tambourine.

(Overlaid by music of orchestra) The tambourine is Spanish. It is used in the symphony orchestra for rhythmic effects in Spanish and Gypsy folk music.

Scene 26

Semi-close-up: Followed by foreground at another angle of performer accompanying same Spanish selection.

Spanish selection.

Scene 27

Pan shot; medium: Same performer goes over to gong.

As a contrast to these—we have the gong—which came to us from the Chinese.

Scene 28

Close-up: Of gong.

The tones of the gong are used for special dramatic, funereal, or weird effects. (Chinese melody is played.)

Scene 29

Medium: Of gong player. Pan to player with triangle.

We now have the triangle. It is equally effective in any key.

Scene 30

Performer plays.

Selection from "Turkish March" by Beethoven.

Scene 31

Semi-close-up: Of lecturer.

These instruments—the triangle, gong, castanets, and tambourine, are used only occasionally in the symphony orchestra.

Scene 32

Semi-close-up: Of player holding cymbals.

The cymbals—The cymbals were in common use among the ancient Egyptians, Assyrians, and Hebrews. They are made of brass wire which is spun into shape and then hammered. Their use is chiefly in highly emphasized rhythms and crashes.

Scene 33

Medium: Of performer playing cymbals.

Selection, excerpt from "Tannhäuser Overture," Wagner.

Scene 34

Semi-close-up: Of lecturer.

The percussion group of the symphony orchestra will play a special arrangement of Schubert's "March Militaire" No. 1.

Scene 35

Series of foreground shots: Showing as each is played, tympani, triangle, bass drum, snare drum, and bells.

Scene 36

General scene. Ensemble finishing selection. Fade out.

APPENDIX C

TYPICAL INITIAL SUBJECT MATTER TEST

AMPHIBIANS

The following is the initial test for the unit Amphibians which was one of the eight units taught in the experiment.

Finish the following statements. Write as much as you can to make the meaning clear. If you cannot finish any statement, skip it and go to the next one. Ready—Begin.

1. The eyes of the frog are protected by

2. Toads are different from frogs because toads

3. The eyes of the tadpole are different from those of the frog because the tadpole's eyes

while the frog's eyes

Complete the following sentences by placing *one* word and *only one* word in each of the spaces. Ready—Begin.

1. The place where the eggs of the frog are laid is in the.......
2. The tadpole breathes by taking in air from the.......
3. The last thing the tadpole loses is its........
4. The frog has......and......which the young tadpole does not have.
5. The part of a frog that is often eaten by man is the.......
6. Tadpoles look like.......
7. Three stages in the life of a frog, in order are......, ..., and ....
8. Young tadpoles breathe by means of.......
9. The tongue of the toad is covered with a......substance.
10. After the tadpole has lost its gills it breathes by means of.......

In each sentence below, choose the word or group of words making a true statement. Then on the dotted line at the right copy the number that is *before* the correct word or words. Ready—Begin.

1. The hind legs of the frog are (1. shorter / 2. longer) than the front legs.   ......

113

2. The feet of the frog are $\left(\begin{array}{l}1.\ \text{hoofed.} \\ 2.\ \text{webbed.}\end{array}\right)$ . . . . . .

3. The first legs to appear on the body of the tadpole are $\left(\begin{array}{l}1.\ \text{hind} \\ 2.\ \text{front}\end{array}\right)$ legs.   . . . . . .

4. Toads usually come out to eat $\left(\begin{array}{l}1.\ \text{at night.} \\ 2.\ \text{in the day time.}\end{array}\right)$ . . . . . .

5. The tongue of the toad is fastened to the mouth $\left(\begin{array}{l}1.\ \text{at the back.} \\ 2.\ \text{in the front.}\end{array}\right)$ . . . . . .

6. Frog's eggs are $\left(\begin{array}{l}1.\ \text{light} \\ 2.\ \text{dark}\end{array}\right)$ in color.   . . . . . .

7. The $\left(\begin{array}{l}1.\ \text{frog} \\ 2.\ \text{toad}\end{array}\right)$ has teeth.   . . . . . .

8. The $\left(\begin{array}{l}1.\ \text{frog} \\ 2.\ \text{toad}\end{array}\right)$ has a slippery skin.   . . . . . .

Four answers are given for each of the following questions. On the dotted line at the right copy the *one* and *only one* number that is before the correct answer. Ready—Begin.

1. Tadpoles are called fish-like because they   . . . . . .
    1. breathe through gills
    2. eat small fish
    3. eat worms
    4. eat mosquito grubs

2. The gills of the tadpole are used for taking   . . . . . .
    1. small insects from the water
    2. small greens from the water
    3. air from the water
    4. small fish from the water

3. The *young* tadpole and frog both have   . . . . . .
    1. lungs
    2. eyes
    3. a long tail
    4. strong legs

4. Of the following, which one always has a long tail?   . . . . . .
    1. toad
    2. turtle
    3. frog
    4. salamander

5. The *young* tadpole has *no* ......
    1. tail
    2. gills
    3. legs
    4. eyes

6. The frog is protected from his enemies by ......
    1. sharp claws
    2. strong hind legs
    3. poisonous fangs
    4. sharp spines

7. Tadpoles eat ......
    1. water plants
    2. tiny fish
    3. water snakes
    4. fish eggs

8. The skin of the frog is ......
    1. covered with hard scales
    2. covered with a hard shell
    3. dry and contains warts
    4. smooth and slippery

9. Frog's eggs are protected by ......
    1. a hard outer shell
    2. a jelly coat
    3. a nest of twigs and straw
    4. being in the ground

10. The *young* tadpole is like the frog in ......
    1. shape of head
    2. being cold-blooded
    3. way of breathing
    4. length of tail

11. The frog hibernates during the ......
    1. winter
    2. summer
    3. autumn
    4. spring

12. Three of the following are enemies of the frog. ......
    Which one is *not* an enemy of the frog?
    1. Owl
    2. Crow
    3. Rat
    4. Snake

13. Hibernating means ......
    1. casting off the skin regularly
    2. sleeping all winter
    3. changing from an egg to a tadpole
    4. changing from a tadpole to a frog

14. The frog is protected from his enemies by   . . . . . .
    1. large strong wings
    2. poisonous warts on his skin
    3. spitting out a brown sticky liquid
    4. taking on the color of his surroundings
15. The gills of the tadpole are   . . . . . .
    1. coiled or curled
    2. dagger-shaped
    3. feather-like
    4. fin-like

If you think the statement below is *True,* place a circle around T at the right of the page. If you think the statement is *False,* place a circle around F at the right of the page. Ready—Begin.

1. The frog develops from a cocoon............................. T   F
2. The feet of the frog are webbed.............................. T   F
3. To kill a toad brings rain .... T   F
4. Toads are usually found on toadstools........................ T   F
5. Salamanders are lizards....................................... T   F
6. The toad is of very great value to the farmer.................. T   F
7. The frog is a cold-blooded animal............................. T   F
8. The bullfrog is an amphibian.................................. T   F
9. Tadpoles eat small insects and worms......................... T   F
10. Tadpoles eat water beetles.................................... T   F
11. If a person touches a toad warts will grow on the hands....... T   F
12. The toad will eat only moving life............................ T   F
13. The tadpole's tail drops off just before it becomes a frog....... T   F

APPENDIX D

TABLES SHOWING COMPLETE DATA

TABLE A
BUTTERFLIES

FINAL TEST		A		B		C		D		E		COMBINED CITIES	
		Exp.	Cont.	Exp.	Cont.	Exp.	Cont.	Exp.	Cont.	Exp.	Cont.	Exp.	Cont.
	No. of Cases	104	78	92	104	76	95	87	82	104	93	463	452
Initial Test	Med.	20.50	22.17	20.96	22.10	22.84	24.73	19.06	18.88	22.50	23.80	20.93	22.15
	Mean	21.14	21.40	21.34	22.32	22.86	24.94	19.36	18.58	23.12	23.96	21.58	22.36
	Q.	4.20	6.15	3.70	4.59	5.38	4.64	2.50	4.04	3.88	4.56	4.19	4.85
	S.D.Dist.	6.69	7.05	5.49	6.17	6.84	6.94	5.36	6.06	6.23	6.42	6.28	6.90
	S.D.M.	.66	.80	.57	.61	.78	.71	.57	.67	.61	.67	.29	.32
	Diff.Means		.26		.98		2.08		.78		.84		.78
	C.R.		.25		1.18		1.98		.90		.92		1.81
	% Sup.		1.2		4.1		9.1		4.3		3.1		3.6
Complete Final Test	Med.	115.95	101.21	131.93	134.50	126.50	126.57	125.14	89.25	142.17	130.27	129.15	117.75
	Mean	115.25	102.35	130.25	132.25	122.45	123.25	123.00	89.75	139.95	126.15	126.40	116.25
	Q.	18.75	22.92	20.00	21.46	26.88	26.97	21.39	15.07	21.16	17.03	21.86	25.50
	S.D.Dist.	32.40	28.67	29.40	30.17	34.29	31.30	25.72	22.52	23.43	26.38	30.45	32.25
	S.D.M	3.18	3.25	3.07	2.96	3.93	3.21	2.76	2.49	2.30	2.74	1.42	1.52
	Diff.Means	12.90		2.00		.80		33.25		13.80		10.15	
	C.R.	2.84		.47		.14		8.94		3.85		4.88	
	% Sup.	12.6		1.5		0.7		37.0		10.9		8.7	
Complete Final Test— Picture-Unit Items	Mean	74.00	59.65	86.90	75.30	77.50	70.26	79.54	53.42	89.94	76.74	81.74	67.86
	S.D.Dist.	20.77	18.18	20.69	16.90	23.82	18.07	16.87	15.22	14.56	15.88	20.39	19.07
	S.D.M.	2.04	2.06	2.16	1.67	2.73	1.85	1.81	1.68	1.43	1.65	.95	.90
	Diff.Means	14.35		11.60		7.24		26.12		13.20		13.88	
	C.R.	4.95		4.25		2.19		10.57		6.06		10.60	
	% Sup.	24.1		15.4		10.3		48.9		17.2		20.5	

CITIES

TABLE A *(Concluded)*

Final Test	Statistic	A Exp.	A Cont.	B Exp.	B Cont.	C Exp.	C Cont.	D Exp.	D Cont.	E Exp.	E Cont.	Combined Exp.	Combined Cont.
No. of Cases		104	78	92	104	76	95	87	82	104	93	463	452
Complete Final Test—Non-Picture Items	Mean	44.42	42.22	42.70	57.10	44.30	52.94	43.46	36.54	50.02	49.54	44.46	48.38
	S.D.Dist.	10.99	13.35	11.14	16.85	13.88	15.23	11.38	10.53	11.82	12.73	12.91	15.84
	S.D.M.	1.08	1.50	1.16	1.65	1.59	1.56	1.22	1.16	1.16	1.32	.60	.74
	Diff.Means	2.20			14.40		1.35	.85		.48			3.92
	C.R.	1.19			7.13		3.87	4.12		.33			4.13
	% Sup.	5.2			33.7		9.7	8.1		1.0			8.8
Gain—Final Test over Initial Test	Med.	44.25	32.50	55.07	52.13	48.75	46.85	55.95	32.86	59.05	45.60	52.11	41.06
	Mean	43.50	34.41	53.91	51.63	48.63	44.22	53.79	33.21	57.03	41.13	51.39	42.21
	Q.	10.31	8.99	10.30	12.62	10.00	7.23	9.90	6.71	11.34	9.79	10.97	13.17
	S.D.Dist.	15.35	10.72	14.36	16.35	16.21	16.83	13.64	11.49	13.95	16.10	15.48	16.69
	S.D.M.	1.50	1.21	1.50	1.60	1.86	1.73	1.46	1.27	1.37	1.67	.72	.78
	Diff.Means	9.09		2.28		4.41		20.58		15.90		9.18	
	C.R.	4.71		1.04		1.74		10.61		7.36		8.66	
	% Sup.	26.4		4.4		10.0		62.0		38.7		21.7	
Gain—Picture-Unit Items	Mean	26.94	17.92	35.08	23.98	29.92	20.56	32.70	15.32	33.44	22.62	31.60	20.36
	S.D.Dist.	9.62	8.68	10.20	7.82	9.91	9.27	9.05	7.60	8.25	8.50	9.81	8.97
	S.D.M.	.94	.98	1.06	.77	1.14	.95	.97	.84	.81	.88	.46	.42
	Diff.Means	9.02		11.10		9.36		17.38		10.82		11.24	
	C.R.	6.63		8.47		6.32		13.58		9.02		18.13	
	% Sup.	50.3		46.3		45.5		113.4		47.8		55.2	
Gain—Non-Picture Items	Mean	16.70	15.92	18.70	27.82	18.93	24.44	21.08	17.72	23.62	21.86	19.84	22.00
	S.D.Dist.	9.50	8.24	7.81	10.84	9.53	9.74	7.85	8.65	8.16	10.06	8.94	10.58
	S.D.M.	.93	.93	.81	1.06	1.09	1.00	.84	.96	.80	1.04	.42	.50

		96	73	81	86	71	87	76	77	95	85	419	408
	Diff.Means	.78			9.12		5.51	3.36		1.76			2.16
	C.R.	.59			6.86		3.72	2.63		1.34			3.32
	% Sup.	4.9			48.8		29.1	19.0		8.1			10.9
Recall Test	No. of Cases	96	73	81	86	71	87	76	77	95	85	419	408
Recall Test Scores	Med.	52.21	42.85	52.00	53.87	52.00	59.00	53.50	45.33	58.75	54.44	54.02	51.17
	Mean	51.04	43.96	54.37	53.80	52.84	59.53	53.38	45.07	60.31	55.96	54.52	52.12
	Q.	12.14	7.37	12.40	9.81	10.58	14.16	9.37	8.39	8.96	10.91	10.77	10.75
	S.D.Dist.	16.10	13.14	16.55	13.63	15.18	17.31	13.89	13.98	14.01	15.15	15.54	15.87
	S.D.M.	1.64	1.54	1.84	1.47	1.80	1.86	1.59	1.59	1.44	1.64	.76	.79
	Diff.Means	7.08		.57			6.69	8.31		4.35		2.40	
	C.R.	3.15		.24			2.58	3.69		2.00		2.18	
	% Sup.	16.1		1.1			12.7	18.4		7.8		4.6	
Recall Test Gain	Med.	30.50	21.95	32.00	31.50	27.00	31.85	33.83	25.40	37.12	30.44	31.96	28.93
	Mean	30.05	22.85	33.11	32.00	29.84	34.37	33.71	27.14	37.04	32.42	32.87	30.05
	Q.	9.08	6.88	9.86	8.53	9.94	10.42	7.31	8.01	7.65	11.59	9.58	9.63
	S.D.Dist.	12.74	12.52	15.90	13.06	13.35	14.52	12.75	12.87	12.18	15.72	13.62	14.43
	S.D.M.	1.30	1.47	1.77	1.41	1.58	1.56	1.46	1.47	1.25	1.70	.67	.71
	Diff.Means	7.20		1.11			4.53	6.57		4.62		2.82	
	C.R.	3.67		.49			2.04	3.17		2.19		2.88	
	% Sup.	31.5		3.5			30.4	24.2		14.3		9.4	
Recall Gain—Picture-Unit Items	Mean	18.68	11.84	20.58	16.64	18.30	15.88	19.86	13.48	20.36	17.26	19.58	15.16
	S.D.Dist.	9.52	9.16	10.38	6.82	8.50	8.38	8.34	7.20	7.18	8.72	8.90	8.32
	S.D.M.	.97	1.07	1.15	.74	1.01	.90	.96	.82	.74	.95	.43	.41
	Diff.Means	6.84		3.94		2.42		6.38		3.10		4.42	
	C.R.	4.75		2.88		1.79		5.06		2.58		7.49	
	% Sup.	57.8		23.7		15.2		27.3		18.0		29.2	
Recall Gain—Non-Picture Items	Mean	11.48	11.18	12.58	15.34	11.54	18.60	14.00	14.72	16.62	15.14	13.32	14.94
	S.D.Dist.	7.32	7.38	7.84	8.16	7.58	8.84	7.40	7.94	7.26	9.20	7.66	8.70
	S.D.M.	.75	.86	.87	.88	.90	.95	.85	.90	.74	.99	.37	.43
	Diff.Means	.30			2.76		7.06		.72	1.48			1.62
	C.R.	.26			2.23		5.39		.59	1.19			2.84
	% Sup.	2.7			21.9		61.2		5.1	9.8			12.2

TABLE B
BEETLES

FINAL TEST			A Exp.	A Cont.	B Exp.	B Cont.	C Exp.	C Cont.	D Exp.	D Cont.	E Exp.	E Cont.	COMBINED CITIES Exp.	COMBINED CITIES Cont.
		No. of Cases	100	77	82	101	70	98	85	87	96	97	433	460
Initial Test		Med.	16.66	16.31	16.50	17.44	17.50	18.07	14.33	13.71	18.88	19.88	16.96	17.12
		Mean	16.99	17.39	17.32	18.02	17.59	18.24	15.01	13.70	21.43	19.39	17.55	17.43
		Q.	3.70	3.60	3.58	3.56	4.00	3.83	3.94	2.86	4.27	4.14	4.36	3.86
		S.D.Dist.	5.65	5.77	5.19	5.98	5.40	5.24	5.68	4.58	8.61	5.72	6.69	5.82
		S.D.M.	.56	.66	.57	.60	.65	.53	.62	.49	.88	.58	.32	.27
		Diff.Means		.40		.70		.65	1.31		2.04		.12	
		C.R.		.46		.84		.77	.52		1.94		.30	
		% Sup.		2.4		4.0		3.7	9.6		10.5		0.7	
Complete Final Test		Med.	105.50	84.75	124.66	124.11	106.75	101.50	112.30	77.25	129.90	113.40	118.00	99.25
		Mean	104.25	87.10	124.20	118.40	110.45	102.35	104.10	72.65	128.55	112.20	114.45	99.75
		Q.	25.20	19.81	20.04	22.14	23.16	24.00	25.85	19.80	17.25	17.31	22.30	23.55
		S.D Dist.	32.93	27.60	25.45	28.53	30.59	31.63	35.10	23.27	24.65	21.48	31.80	31.61
		S.D.M.	3.29	3.15	2.81	2.84	3.66	3.20	3.81	2.49	2.52	2.18	1.53	1.47
		Diff.Means	17.15		5.80		8.10		31.45		16.35		14.70	
		C.R.	3.81		1.45		1.67		6.91		4.91		6.93	
		% Sup.	19.7		4.9		7.9		43.3		14.6		14.7	
Complete Final Test—Picture-Unit Items		Mean	60.85	43.40	70.95	62.35	63.20	50.35	59.45	35.55	75.30	57.80	66.05	50.60
		S.D.Dist	19.23	15.45	14.65	15.30	19.44	17.52	20.50	12.37	16.26	13.87	19.23	17.85
		S.D.M.	1.92	1.76	1.62	1.52	2.32	1.77	2.22	1.33	1.66	1.41	.92	.83

Item / Statistic												
Diff.Means	17.45		8.60		3.85		23.90		17.50		15.45	
C.R.	6.71		3.87		4.40		9.23		8.03		12.46	
% Sup.	40.2		13.8		6.5		67.2		30.3		30.5	
Complete Final Test— Non-Picture Items												
Mean	43.85	43.65	53.45	56.20	47.05	52.05	44.90	37.10	53.05	47.95	48.45	49.25
S.D.Dist.	16.08	14.35	12.40	14.99	13.58	15.72	16.65	13.64	11.49	16.42	14.75	15.78
S.D.M.	1.61	1.64	1.37	1.49	1.62	1.59	1.81	1.46	1.17	1.67	.71	.74
Diff.Means	.20			2.75		5.00	7.80		5.10			.80
C.R.	.09			1.36		2.20	3.35		2.50			.78
% Sup.	0.5			5.1		10.6	21.0		10.6			1.7
Gain— Final Test Over Initial Test												
Med.	40.50	28.32	51.00	48.13	39.15	36.30	44.13	25.68	47.43	44.37	44.90	36.42
Mean	40.56	29.65	49.76	46.50	40.50	36.72	41.94	24.60	47.13	42.42	44.01	36.60
Q.	11.81	10.38	11.10	9.63	12.55	12.54	12.35	9.75	7.97	8.39	11.54	11.61
S.D.Dist.	18.97	13.56	14.77	12.81	17.06	15.57	17.87	12.24	13.46	14.25	16.25	15.92
S.D.M.	1.90	1.55	1.63	1.27	2.04	1.57	1.94	1.31	1.37	1.45	.78	.74
Diff.Means	10.91		3.26		3.78		17.34		4.71		7.41	
C.R.	4.45		1.55		1.47		7.41		2.37		6.86	
% Sup.	36.8		7.0		10.3		70.5		11.1		20.2	
Gain— Picture-Unit Items												
Mean	23.48	12.00	26.54	21.36	21.84	16.10	23.32	9.22	24.50	18.82	23.98	15.84
S.D.Dist.	9.46	8.01	10.12	7.44	10.64	9.88	11.30	6.30	9.68	8.46	10.34	9.26
S.D.M.	.95	.91	1.12	.74	1.27	1.00	1.23	.68	.99	.86	.50	.43
Diff.Means	11.48		5.18		5.74		14.10		5.68		8.14	
C.R.	8.70		3.87		3.54		10.00		4.34		12.33	
% Sup.	95.7		24.3		35.7		152.9		30.2		51.4	
Gain— Non-Picture Items												
Mean	18.16	17.78	23.74	24.98	18.64	20.74	18.74	15.48	22.58	23.30	20.40	20.72
S.D.Dist.	8.88	8.02	6.76	7.70	8.44	7.12	8.78	8.04	6.46	8.64	8.22	8.64
S.D.M.	.89	.91	.75	.77	1.01	.72	.95	.86	.66	.88	.40	.40
Diff.Means	.38			1.24		2.10	3.26			.72		.32
C.R.	.30			1.16		1.69	2.55			.65		.56
% Sup.	2.1			5.2		11.3	21.1			3.2		1.6

TABLE B (*Concluded*)

RECALL TEST		A Exp.	A Cont.	B Exp.	B Cont.	C Exp.	C Cont.	D Exp.	D Cont.	E Exp.	E Cont.	Combined Cities Exp.	Combined Cities Cont.
No. of Cases		94	71	73	81	66	88	76	80	89	90	398	410
Recall Test Scores	Med.	45.50	30.90	48.50	50.33	37.10	41.50	42.50	30.64	49.75	44.90	45.38	39.82
	Mean	43.88	32.86	48.18	48.70	39.10	42.50	41.16	32.10	50.88	44.78	44.92	40.52
	Q.	10.20	7.68	12.73	9.29	9.07	10.66	13.15	7.67	8.48	7.98	10.75	10.59
	S.D.Dist.	14.55	11.86	14.65	13.08	13.84	14.56	15.90	11.12	11.60	10.64	14.79	13.96
	S.D.M.	1.50	1.41	1.71	1.45	1.70	1.55	1.82	1.24	1.23	1.12	.74	.69
	Diff.Means	11.02			.52		3.40	9.06		6.10		4.40	
	C.R.	5.35			.23		1.48	4.12		3.67		4.36	
	% Sup.	33.5			1.2		8.7	28.2		13.6		10.9	
Recall Test Gain	Med.	27.50	14.36	33.50	31.90	20.17	23.17	25.70	16.21	29.50	25.93	27.30	21.80
	Mean	27.00	15.04	31.98	30.74	21.28	24.04	26.08	18.58	29.32	25.14	27.18	22.98
	Q.	8.40	6.00	10.97	9.00	8.66	10.50	10.41	7.61	6.87	7.98	9.63	9.58
	S.D.Dist.	12.66	10.16	13.82	12.32	13.78	14.04	15.78	11.88	10.88	11.40	13.75	13.20
	S.D.M.	1.31	1.21	1.62	1.37	1.70	1.50	1.81	1.33	1.15	1.20	.69	.65
	Diff.Means	11.96		.54			2.76	7.50		4.18		4.20	
	C.R.	6.72		.25			1.22	3.33		2.52		4.42	
	% Sup.	79.5		1.8			13.0	40.4		16.6		18.3	
Recall Gain— Picture-Unit Items	Mean	19.12	8.78	20.94	18.26	15.28	12.64	15.48	8.32	18.72	13.92	18.04	12.52
	S.D.Dist.	9.32	7.48	11.05	7.15	10.07	9.38	10.39	7.61	8.07	7.91	9.95	8.75
	S.D.M.	.96	.89	1.29	.79	1.24	1.00	1.19	.85	.86	.83	.50	.43
	Diff.Means	10.34		2.68		2.64		7.16		4.80		5.52	
	C.R.	7.89		1.77		1.66		4.90		4.00		8.49	
	% Sup.	117.8		14.7		20.9		86.1		34.5		44.1	
Recall Gain— Non-Picture Items	Mean	7.96	6.20	10.18	12.48	6.10	11.70	10.48	10.46	10.54	11.22	9.12	10.54
	S.D.Dist.	5.77	5.16	5.59	7.72	5.58	7.07	7.53	6.71	5.60	6.24	6.27	7.02
	S.D.M.	.60	.61	.65	.86	.69	.75	.86	.75	.59	.66	.31	.35
	Diff.Means	1.76			2.30		5.60	.02			.68		1.42
	C.R.	2.05			2.13		5.49	.02			.76		3.02
	% Sup.	28.4			22.6		91.8	0.2			6.5		15.6

TABLE C
AMPHIBIANS

FINAL TEST		A Exp.	A Cont.	B Exp.	B Cont.	C Exp.	C Cont.	D Exp.	D Cont.	E Exp.	E Cont.	Combined Exp.	Combined Cont.
No. of Cases		104	76	84	97	76	95	72	81	102	105	438	454
Initial Test	Med.	28.04	28.16	31.64	33.00	29.18	31.20	22.66	22.26	36.25	36.62	29.44	31.00
	Mean	28.80	29.38	31.86	33.06	30.48	33.48	23.98	22.76	37.02	36.72	30.62	31.86
	Q.	6.70	7.86	7.28	6.01	6.70	7.97	4.61	4.13	7.82	8.31	7.30	8.03
	S.D.Dist.	10.58	10.93	9.47	9.63	10.61	11.43	7.19	8.17	11.46	11.72	10.96	11.59
	S.D.M.	1.03	1.25	1.03	.98	1.22	1.17	.79	.88	1.13	1.14	.52	.54
	Diff.Means		.12		1.20		3.00	1.22		.30			1.24
	C.R.		.36		.85		1.78	1.03		.19			1.65
	% Sup.		0.4		3.8		9.8	5.4		0.8			4.0
Complete Final Test	Med.	139.25	123.00	149.15	143.40	124.25	140.10	147.80	112.30	157.40	145.15	147.70	133.75
	Mean	131.70	120.75	143.70	137.75	125.50	135.55	146.25	108.10	154.80	142.90	140.80	130.05
	Q.	22.31	22.07	17.10	19.59	26.25	21.33	11.08	18.29	9.60	13.35	17.98	21.05
	S.D.Dist.	32.33	29.92	25.56	27.47	30.68	27.18	17.46	25.47	16.93	18.01	27.57	28.62
	S.D.M.	3.15	3.43	2.79	2.79	3.52	2.79	1.92	2.73	1.68	1.76	1.30	1.33
	Diff.Means	10.95		5.95			10.05	35.50		11.90		10.75	
	C.R.	2.35		1.51			2.24	11.42		4.90		5.78	
	% Sup.	9.1		4.3			8.0	31.6		8.3		8.3	
Complete Final Test— Picture-Unit Items	Mean	80.42	70.34	88.18	80.66	79.14	77.50	92.26	65.78	97.30	83.58	87.66	76.18
	S.D.Dist.	22.77	19.84	16.49	17.93	19.40	19.03	11.55	19.29	11.50	11.83	18.42	18.73
	S.D.M.	2.22	2.28	1.80	1.82	2.23	1.95	1.27	2.07	1.14	1.15	.87	.87
	Diff.Means	10.08		7.52		1.64		26.48		13.72		11.48	
	C.R.	3.17		2.93		.55		10.90		8.47		9.33	
	% Sup.	14.3		9.3		2.1		40.3		16.4		15.1	

TABLE C (*Concluded*)

FINAL TEST	No. of Cases	A Exp.	A Cont.	B Exp.	B Cont.	C Exp.	C Cont.	D Exp.	D Cont.	E Exp.	E Cont.	Combined Exp.	Combined Cont.
		104	76	84	97	76	95	72	81	102	105	438	454
Complete Final Test—Non-Picture Items	Mean	50.98	50.30	55.74	56.98	46.50	57.94	54.22	42.54	57.70	58.98	53.26	53.78
	S.D.Dist.	11.78	11.60	10.49	11.55	12.36	10.00	8.52	9.13	7.48	8.04	10.86	11.85
	S.D.M.	1.15	1.33	1.14	1.17	1.42	1.03	.94	.98	.74	.78	.51	.55
	Diff.Means	.68			1.24		11.44	11.68			1.28		.52
	C.R.	.39			.76		6.54	8.59			1.19		.22
	% Sup.	1.4			2.2		24.6	27.5			2.2		1.0
Gain—Final Test Over Initial Test	Med.	41.40	28.92	43.77	37.26	33.38	32.67	53.20	30.75	45.38	33.27	43.86	32.58
	Mean	39.21	30.63	41.25	35.94	33.78	32.67	52.62	30.54	44.25	32.58	42.30	32.61
	Q.	8.48	9.20	7.71	10.07	9.38	10.12	6.63	7.32	7.87	8.93	9.46	9.46
	S.D.Dist.	14.32	13.19	13.50	14.15	13.16	12.80	10.24	11.66	11.90	12.57	14.03	13.03
	S.D.M.	1.40	1.51	1.47	1.44	1.51	1.31	1.12	1.25	1.18	1.23	.66	.61
	Diff.Means	8.58		5.31		1.11		22.08		11.67		9.69	
	C.R.	4.17		2.58		.56		13.14		6.86		10.77	
	% Sup.	28.0		14.8		3.4		72.3		35.8		29.7	
Gain—Picture-Unit Items	Mean	29.45	21.14	31.04	24.65	26.00	21.53	39.47	22.85	32.06	21.86	31.61	22.46
	S.D.Dist.	11.94	10.77	9.15	12.51	10.56	10.80	8.34	10.50	8.88	9.78	10.77	11.82
	S.D.M.	1.17	1.24	1.00	1.27	1.21	1.11	.92	1.13	.88	.95	.51	.55
	Diff.Means	8.31		6.39		4.47		16.62		10.20		9.15	
	C.R.	4.89		3.94		2.73		11.38		7.91		12.20	
	% Sup.	39.3		25.9		20.8		72.7		46.7		40.7	
Gain—Non-Picture Items	Mean	9.70	9.76	10.30	11.32	7.98	10.98	13.10	7.84	11.78	10.66	10.62	10.18
	S.D.Dist.	5.76	4.52	6.14	4.74	5.52	4.48	4.34	5.28	5.12	5.32	5.68	5.06
	S.D.M.	.56	.52	.67	.48	.63	.46	.48	.57	.51	.52	.27	.24

RECALL TEST		415	416	98	96	82	75	86	71	80	77	69	97
	Diff.Means	.44			1.12	5.26		3.00		1.02		.06	
	C.R.	1.26			1.53	7.01		3.85		1.24		.08	
	% Sup.	4.3			10.5	67.1		37.6		9.9		0.6	
	NO. OF CASES	415	416	98	96	82	75	86	71	80	77	69	97
Recall Test Scores	Med.	62.08	66.40	71.36	74.70	49.50	65.14	64.50	57.85	63.30	67.25	51.00	64.71
	Mean	60.06	64.41	70.47	72.60	50.28	63.09	60.72	58.65	62.19	64.83	53.58	61.23
	Q.	13.99	11.42	8.10	10.85	10.97	10.48	14.28	13.90	11.50	10.61	17.36	10.59
	S.D.Dist.	17.75	16.00	13.20	13.47	16.03	14.14	17.19	17.22	16.35	14.64	18.72	17.61
	S.D.M.	.87	.78	1.33	1.37	1.77	1.63	1.85	2.04	1.83	1.67	2.25	1.79
	Diff.Means		4.32		2.13		12.81	2.07			2.64		7.65
	C.R.		3.69		1.12		5.32	.75			1.06		2.66
	% Sup.		7.2		3.0		25.5	3.5			4.2		14.3
Recall Test Gain	Med.	28.04	33.90	34.00	33.10	25.37	40.37	27.83	26.20	30.35	32.80	24.14	34.00
	Mean	28.78	33.37	34.12	35.02	27.85	39.19	26.71	27.40	29.05	32.80	24.61	32.08
	Q.	10.10	9.58	10.21	9.21	9.50	7.90	10.20	11.09	9.25	8.61	8.95	8.80
	S.D.Dist.	14.81	13.91	15.68	13.80	15.08	12.39	14.04	14.37	13.76	11.21	12.96	14.62
	S.D.M.	.73	.68	1.58	1.41	1.67	1.43	1.51	1.70	1.54	1.28	1.56	1.48
	Diff.Means		4.59		.90		11.34		.69		3.75		7.47
	C.R.		4.59		.42		5.15		.30		1.88		3.47
	% Sup.		15.9		2.6		40.7		2.6		12.9		30.4
Recall Gain—Picture-Unit Items	Mean	19.57	24.88	19.15	25.87	19.66	28.93	17.89	20.95	19.60	23.47	17.44	24.82
	S.D.Dist.	11.46	11.04	14.91	10.59	10.50	10.11	11.28	11.70	11.67	8.79	10.62	11.82
	S.D.M.	.56	.54	1.51	1.08	1.16	1.17	1.22	1.39	1.30	1.00	1.28	1.20
	Diff.Means		5.31		6.72		9.27		3.06		3.87		7.38
	C.R.		6.81		3.61		5.62		1.65		2.36		4.22
	% Sup.		27.1		35.1		47.2		17.1		19.7		42.3
Recall Gain—Non-Picture Items	Mean	9.26	8.46	11.41	9.05	8.26	9.97	8.94	6.94	9.46	9.18	7.54	7.26
	S.D.Dist.	5.57	5.36	5.36	5.58	6.15	4.92	5.12	5.60	5.23	4.91	5.13	5.08
	S.D.M.	.27	.26	.54	.57	.68	.57	.55	.66	.58	.56	.62	.52
	Diff.Means	.80		2.36			1.71	2.00		.28		.28	
	C.R.	2.16		2.99			1.92	2.33		.35		.35	
	% Sup.	9.5		26.1			20.7	28.8		3.1		3.9	

TABLE D

GROWTH OF PLANTS

		CITIES										COMBINED CITIES	
		A		B		C		D		E			
FINAL TEST		Exp.	Cont.	Exp.	Cont.	Exp.	Cont.	Exp.	Cont.	Exp.	Cont.	Exp.	Cont.
	No. of Cases	107	77	92	104	77	100	88	85	100	108	464	474
Initial Test	Med.	21.72	23.72	28.00	27.92	27.30	34.30	24.32	26.00	31.08	35.40	26.24	29.53
	Mean	23.04	24.18	28.96	29.38	27.14	34.70	27.50	26.00	32.46	35.40	27.76	30.42
	Q.	4.91	4.98	6.53	7.57	6.07	7.67	8.61	8.58	7.27	8.32	6.88	7.91
	S.D.Dist.	8.50	7.50	9.29	10.25	8.81	10.14	11.82	10.70	11.24	11.47	10.54	11.14
	S.D.M.	.82	.85	.97	1.00	1.00	1.01	1.26	1.16	1.12	1.10	.49	.51
	Diff.Means		1.14		.42		7.56	1.50			2.94		2.66
	C.R.		.94		.30		5.32	.88			1.87		3.75
	% Sup.		4.9		1.5		27.9	5.8			9.1		9.6
Complete Final Test	Med.	87.30	79.00	107.15	120.50	104.65	110.50	104.67	70.92	124.25	101.75	106.19	96.22
	Mean	88.80	82.35	105.00	111.55	102.05	108.95	104.15	69.60	121.50	103.45	104.15	96.90
	Q.	26.40	20.08	18.25	22.32	17.97	25.97	18.57	18.92	20.82	12.75	21.38	23.86
	S.D.Dist.	33.09	28.39	26.38	29.88	26.00	30.81	24.15	22.77	25.54	20.52	29.61	31.14
	S.D.M.	3.20	3.24	2.75	2.93	2.96	3.08	2.57	2.47	2.55	1.97	1.37	1.43
	Diff.Means	6.45			6.55		6.90	34.55		18.05		7.25	
	C.R.	1.42			1.63		1.62	9.71		5.61		3.66	
	% Sup.	7.8			6.2		6.8	49.6		17.4		7.5	
Complete Final Test—Picture-Unit Items	Mean	60.09	55.82	72.10	68.10	66.18	68.22	70.10	44.82	80.66	65.42	69.82	61.34
	S.D.Dist.	22.70	17.49	17.47	18.92	16.13	20.04	15.40	13.51	16.51	13.02	19.39	19.03
	S.D.M.	2.19	1.99	1.82	1.86	1.84	2.00	1.64	1.47	1.65	1.25	.90	.87

	C1	C2	C3	C4	C5	C6	C7	C8	C9	C10	C11	C12
Diff.Means	4.27		4.00			2.04	25.28		15.24		8.48	
C.R.	1.44		1.54			.75	11.49		7.36		6.78	
% Sup.	7.6		5.9			3.1	56.4		23.3		13.8	
Complete Final Test—Non-Picture Items												
Mean	28.70	27.38	32.78	43.14	35.66	40.58	34.16	24.24	40.54	38.14	34.26	35.52
S.D.Dist.	12.96	12.75	11.26	12.60	11.60	12.70	11.09	11.80	10.90	10.09	12.29	14.05
S.D.M.	1.25	1.45	1.17	1.24	1.32	1.27	1.18	1.28	1.09	.97	.57	.65
Diff.Means	1.32			10.36		4.92	9.92		2.40			1.26
C.R.	.69			6.09		2.69	5.70		1.60			1.47
% Sup.	4.8			31.6		13.8	40.9		6.3			3.7
Gain—Final Test Over Initial Test												
Med.	35.64	27.60	42.51	51.38	41.63	39.50	42.30	17.40	45.50	31.83	43.77	32.62
Mean	33.01	29.82	39.96	46.08	41.19	37.47	43.71	19.59	45.12	31.37	40.83	33.51
Q.	15.39	12.73	11.79	15.75	13.69	14.00	12.42	9.47	10.77	10.05	13.85	16.01
S.D.Dist.	20.78	20.93	17.67	20.39	18.56	18.89	18.35	13.97	14.69	16.79	18.55	20.31
S.D.M.	2.01	2.39	1.84	2.00	2.11	1.89	1.96	1.52	1.47	1.62	.86	.93
Diff.Means	3.19			6.12	3.72		24.12		13.75		7.32	
C.R.	1.02			2.25	1.31		9.73		6.30		5.76	
% Sup.	10.7			15.3	9.9		123.1		43.8		21.8	
Gain—Picture-Unit Items												
Mean	20.00	15.68	21.92	18.80	19.19	13.13	22.73	6.65	20.45	9.44	20.42	12.77
S.D.Dist.	13.14	12.48	11.34	13.17	12.30	10.59	12.51	9.69	10.56	12.18	13.08	12.54
S.D.M.	1.27	1.42	1.18	1.29	1.40	1.06	1.33	1.05	1.06	1.17	.61	.58
Diff.Means	4.32		3.12		6.06		16.08		11.01		7.65	
C.R.	2.26		1.78		3.48		9.51		6.97		9.11	
% Sup.	27.6		16.6		46.2		241.8		116.6		59.9	
Gain—Non-Picture Items												
Mean	15.04	14.94	17.98	27.14	22.12	25.28	21.54	13.00	24.02	22.12	19.96	21.08
S.D.Dist.	10.80	11.10	10.06	10.40	9.80	10.54	10.08	10.60	8.80	8.32	10.50	11.54
S.D.M.	1.04	1.26	1.05	1.02	1.12	1.05	1.07	1.18	.88	.80	.49	.53
Diff.Means	.10			9.16		3.16	8.54		1.90			1.12
C.R.	.06			6.27		2.05	5.37		1.60			1.56
% Sup.	0.7			50.9		14.3	65.7		8.6			5.6

TABLE D (*Concluded*)

Recall Test		A Exp.	A Cont.	B Exp.	B Cont.	C Exp.	C Cont.	D Exp.	D Cont.	E Exp.	E Cont.	Combined Cities Exp.	Combined Cities Cont.
	No. of Cases	99	70	84	88	72	92	81	81	95	102	431	433
Recall Test Scores	Med.	57.00	47.50	61.00	72.00	59.50	69.30	61.00	47.55	73.87	63.50	62.16	61.30
	Mean	54.33	52.83	61.14	68.85	60.87	66.36	60.33	46.26	71.43	64.23	61.65	59.73
	Q.	18.45	17.07	14.02	15.86	14.10	13.12	11.45	13.50	13.90	14.62	14.88	14.88
	S.D.Dist.	22.44	22.47	19.44	21.60	18.69	19.62	16.92	15.48	18.63		20.28	21.60
	S.D.M.	2.26	2.69	2.12	2.30	2.20	2.05	1.88	1.72	1.91	1.45	.98	1.04
	Diff.Means	1.50			7.71		5.49	14.07		7.20		1.92	
	C.R.	.43			2.46		1.82	5.52		3.01		1.34	
	% Sup.	2.8			12.6		9.0	30.4		11.2		3.2	
Recall Test Gain	Med.	32.87	25.00	29.50	41.50	31.75	32.50	32.29	19.33	39.62	26.50	33.48	28.06
	Mean	31.36	28.87	31.81	39.70	33.37	31.78	32.26	20.38	38.41	28.93	33.52	30.10
	Q.	15.77	14.43	15.00	15.30	14.38	11.75	11.51	8.42	12.51	10.33	13.30	13.05
	S.D.Dist.	20.82	20.16	17.70	20.22	18.63	17.10	17.22	13.18	17.40	7.89	18.63	18.40
	S.D.M.	2.09	2.41	1.93	2.16	2.19	1.78	1.91	1.46	1.79	.78	.90	.88
	Diff.Means	2.49			7.89	1.59		11.88		9.48		3.42	
	C.R.	.78			2.72	.56		4.95		4.86		2.71	
	% Sup.	8.6			24.8	5.0		58.3		32.8		11.4	
Recall Gain—Picture-Unit Items	Mean	17.89	14.56	14.65	16.51	14.14	9.91	13.84	6.52	17.92	9.25	15.88	11.23
	S.D.Dist.	13.05	13.44	12.09	13.17	11.91	11.37	14.04	10.02	13.02	11.55	12.99	12.42
	S.D.M.	1.31	1.61	1.32	1.40	1.40	1.19	1.56	1.11	1.34	1.14	.63	.60
	Diff.Means	3.33			1.86	4.23		7.32		8.67		4.65	
	C.R.	1.60			.97	2.30		3.83		4.93		5.34	
	% Sup.	22.9			12.7	42.7		112.27		93.7		41.4	
Recall Gain—Non-Picture Items	Mean	13.52	14.36	17.38	22.96	19.20	22.00	18.26	13.80	20.60	19.70	17.66	18.88
	S.D.Dist.	10.68	10.40	9.10	9.88	8.62	9.92	9.14	9.52	7.82	7.24	9.58	10.08
	S.D.M.	1.07	1.24	.99	1.05	1.02	1.03	1.02	1.06	.80	.72	.46	.48
	Diff.Means		.84		5.58		2.80	4.46		.90			1.22
	C.R.		.51		3.88		1.93	3.03		.83			1.85
	% Sup.		6.2		32.1		14.6	32.3		4.6			6.9

TABLE E
TOTAL SCIENCE TEST

FINAL TEST		A Exp.	A Cont.	B Exp.	B Cont.	C Exp.	C Cont.	D Exp.	D Cont.	E Exp.	E Cont.	COMBINED CITIES Exp.	COMBINED CITIES Cont.
	No. of Cases	93	66	68	82	63	79	60	70	81	70	365	367
Chronological Ages (in months)	Med.	126.63	130.50	131.50	132.00	129.15	129.54	127.05	129.96	127.08	126.38	128.07	129.39
	Mean	127.79	131.47	132.40	132.77	128.46	129.33	129.00	130.89	127.74	127.62	129.90	131.40
	Q.	6.04	6.67	6.60	7.38	5.14	6.30	4.56	4.24	3.93	3.58	5.19	5.97
	S.D.Dist.	11.54	9.20	10.92	11.30	10.54	10.45	8.24	8.40	7.53	6.81	10.16	9.74
	S.D.M.	1.20	1.12	1.32	1.25	1.33	1.18	1.12	1.04	.84	.81	.54	.51
	Diff.Means		3.68		.37		.87		1.89		.12		1.50
	C.R.		2.24		.20		.49		1.24		.10		2.03
	% Sup.		2.9		0.3		0.7		1.5		0.1		1.2
Intelligence Quotient	Med.	105.82	103.30	101.30	102.50	101.66	105.50	104.50	95.05	112.36	111.57	105.77	103.20
	Mean	105.46	103.10	101.22	102.26	104.30	105.58	103.38	94.22	112.78	111.86	105.78	103.54
	Q.	11.11	12.16	8.04	8.58	8.28	10.77	9.58	7.12	7.73	7.07	9.44	10.00
	S.D.Dist.	18.07	18.12	11.97	15.52	14.90	18.34	16.28	10.81	13.35	11.96	15.76	16.37
	S.D.M.	1.87	2.20	1.45	1.71	1.88	2.06	2.22	1.34	1.48	1.43	.83	.86
	Diff.Means		2.36		1.04		1.28		9.16		.92		2.24
	C.R.		.82		.46		.46		3.54		.45		1.88
	% Sup.		2.3		1.0		1.2		9.7		0.8		2.2
Initial Test	Med.	87.80	89.50	96.20	100.50	96.12	107.37	79.50	78.50	110.92	116.21	94.38	99.93
	Mean	90.35	87.25	100.15	102.15	98.50	108.90	85.35	80.80	115.45	115.35	98.35	100.65
	Q.	15.05	16.62	15.50	14.37	14.11	16.32	17.23	16.60	21.54	15.54	17.63	18.23
	S.D.Dist.	25.35	25.62	22.49	24.30	23.18	27.99	24.74	21.41	32.17	23.56	28.07	26.92

TABLE E (Continued)

		CITIES										COMBINED CITIES	
		A		B		C		D		E			
FINAL TEST		Exp.	Cont.	Exp.	Cont.	Exp.	Cont.	Exp.	Cont.	Exp.	Cont.	Exp.	Cont.
No. of Cases		93	66	68	82	63	79	60	70	81	70	365	367
	S.D.M.	2.63	3.15	2.73	2.68	2.92	3.15	3.19	2.56	3.57	2.82	1.47	1.41
	Diff.Means	3.10			2.00		10.40	4.55		.10			2.30
	C.R.	.76			.52		2.42	1.11		.02			1.13
	% Sup.	3.6			2.0		10.6	5.6		0.1			2.3
Final Test I (Items Equivalent to Initial Test)	Med.	248.64	203.50	296.83	290.16	281.50	268.50	283.50	184.83	306.93	265.21	286.36	243.83
	Mean	246.46	216.10	292.44	279.79	267.02	258.14	280.70	190.58	309.52	267.50	278.70	244.30
	Q.	47.75	47.17	36.67	50.50	48.50	61.00	32.00	34.00	33.78	34.86	41.47	52.19
	S.D Dist.	71.92	64.48	55.37	62.74	66.28	67.87	48.61	45.46	45.07	40.94	63.56	66.75
	S.D.M.	7.38	7.94	6.71	6.93	8.35	7.64	6.28	5.43	5.01	4.89	3.33	3.48
	Diff.Means	30.36		12.65		8.88		90.12		42.02		34.40	
	C.R.	2.80		1.31		.78		10.86		6.00		4.82	
	% Sup.	14.0		4.5		3.4		47.3		15.7		14.1	
Complete Final Test	Med.	463.00	372.95	518.00	516.50	478.25	473.94	476.15	351.95	563.00	486.50	499.11	437.23
	Mean	443.45	388.70	516.89	495.50	464.00	463.10	478.55	344.60	551.45	487.10	500.40	438.95
	Q.	86.43	73.20	60.00	88.12	82.03	104.10	46.87	63.56	55.83	47.49	75.25	90.90
	S.D.Dist.	126.15	107.27	94.97	109.85	111.65	118.64	78.56	78.84	78.98	68.84	109.35	115.38
	S.D.M.	13.08	13.20	11.52	12.13	14.07	13.35	10.14	9.42	8.78	8.23	5.72	6.02
	Diff.Means	54.75		21.39		.90		133.95		64.35		61.45	
	C.R.	2.95		1.28		.05		9.68		5.35		7.40	
	% Sup.	14.1		4.3		0.2		38.9		13.2		14.0	
Complete Final Test	Mean	277.45	227.65	327.10	283.45	288.70	262.45	301.45	202.45	346.60	284.35	307.90	253.60

Picture-Unit Items

S.D.Dist.	80.91	65.64	59.01	62.69	70.55	70.24	49.58	46.89	44.87	41.76	69.02	66.98
S.D.M.	8.39	8.08	7.16	6.92	8.89	7.90	6.45	5.60	4.99	4.99	3.62	3.50
Diff.Means	49.80		43.65		26.25		99.00		62.25		54.30	
C.R.	4.27		4.38		2.21		11.59		9.80		10.78	
% Sup.	21.9		15.4		10.0		48.9		21.9		21.4	

Complete Final Test Non-Picture Items

Mean	167.20	163.00	189.50	211.90	176.10	202.70	179.20	143.10	204.00	203.40	183.00	186.40
S.D.Dist.	48.88	44.24	38.13	51.36	44.59	51.68	34.11	35.32	32.66	31.08	42.92	51.45
S.D.M.	5.07	5.45	4.62	5.67	5.62	5.81	4.44	4.22	3.63	3.71	2.25	2.69
Diff.Means	4.20			22.40		26.60	36.10		.60			3.40
C.R.	.56			3.06		3.29	5.89		.12			.97
% Sup.	2.6			11.8		15.1	25.2		0.3			1.9

Gain—Final Test over Initial Test

Med.	162.50	118.50	193.86	184.50	177.30	157.62	194.50	102.50	191.93	148.50	185.57	141.50
Mean	157.62	124.10	193.46	177.38	168.82	146.34	194.90	108.58	191.86	150.66	179.94	142.90
Q	39.97	35.82	33.80	40.60	42.16	47.20	28.27	29.75	24.89	28.80	35.06	43.26
S.D.Dist.	58.18	49.10	46.27	54.29	56.30	52.33	41.74	36.79	36.70	42.30	51.47	53.38
S.D.M.	6.03	6.04	5.61	6.00	7.09	5.89	5.39	4.40	4.08	5.06	2.69	2.79
Diff.Means	33.52		16.08		22.48		86.32		41.20		37.04	
C.R.	3.93		1.96		2.44		12.40		6.34		9.55	
% Sup.	27.0		9.1		15.4		79.5		27.3		25.9	

Gain—Picture-Unit Items

Mean	99.26	66.14	118.22	87.42	96.22	69.66	117.74	55.58	111.18	73.18	107.90	71.02
S.D.Dist.	35.04	31.04	29.44	31.20	35.04	27.44	26.00	20.16	23.36	26.88	31.76	29.44
S.D.M.	3.63	3.82	3.57	3.45	4.41	3.09	3.36	2.41	2.60	3.21	1.66	1.54
Diff.Means	33.12		30.80		26.56		62.16		38.00		36.88	
C.R.	6.28		6.21		4.94		15.05		9.20		16.32	
% Sup.	50.1		35.2		38.1		111.8		51.9		51.9	

Gain—Non-Picture Items

Mean	58.90	57.22	73.96	90.16	69.76	82.12	77.20	55.30	83.38	79.36	72.04	73.18
S.D.Dist.	26.82	22.20	20.76	27.24	25.92	25.62	20.70	23.10	17.70	20.10	24.42	27.54
S.D.M.	2.78	2.73	2.52	3.01	3.27	2.88	2.67	2.76	1.97	2.40	1.28	1.44
Diff.Means	1.68			16.20		12.36	21.90		4.02			1.14
C.R.	.43			4.12		2.83	5.70		1.30			.59
% Sup.	2.9			21.9		17.7	39.6		5.1			1.6

TABLE E (Concluded)

RECALL TEST		A Exp.	A Cont.	B Exp.	B Cont.	C Exp.	C Cont.	D Exp.	D Cont.	E Exp.	E Cont.	COMBINED CITIES Exp.	COMBINED CITIES Cont.
No. of Cases		86	60	63	71	61	74	55	66	76	64	341	335
Recall Test Scores	Med.	222.50	174.50	236.10	234.50	211.50	224.50	221.70	174.50	256.10	233.17	232.97	211.00
	Mean	210.42	181.46	234.74	230.34	213.38	227.46	221.30	176.58	256.42	233.22	227.46	210.90
	Q.	48.50	43.33	37.75	46.50	43.70	50.20	36.16	36.00	36.00	31.34	39.39	46.19
	S.D.Dist.	65.29	58.88	60.18	60.13	59.63	62.51	52.90	46.53	46.61	45.04	60.16	60.72
	S.D.M.	7.04	7.60	7.58	7.14	7.64	7.27	7.13	5.73	5.35	5.63	3.26	3.32
	Diff.Means	28.96		4.40			14.08	44.72		23.20		16.56	
	C.R.	2.80		.42			1.33	4.89		2.99		3.56	
	% Sup.	16.0		1.9			6.6	25.3		9.9		7.9	
Recall Test Gain	Med.	129.83	80.50	137.83	133.50	108.50	116.50	130.50	91.93	136.50	114.10	128.70	107.61
	Mean	120.10	88.10	134.42	128.66	114.42	115.62	134.50	98.90	140.18	120.66	128.50	111.14
	Q.	36.57	27.00	41.33	45.10	28.50	34.51	32.83	26.05	25.33	33.20	31.42	37.49
	S.D.Dist.	50.24	44.72	49.12	52.54	48.88	46.30	46.87	45.77	37.11	46.39	47.71	49.49
	S.D.M.	5.42	5.77	6.19	6.24	6.26	5.38	6.32	5.63	4.26	5.80	2.58	2.70
	Diff.Means	32.00		5.76			1.20	35.60		19.52		17.36	
	C.R.	4.04		.66			.15	4.21		2.71		4.65	
	% Sup.	36.3		4.5			1.0	36.0		16.2		15.6	
Recall Gain— Picture-Unit Items	Mean	79.66	49.90	82.70	70.22	69.90	54.86	79.74	50.38	83.26	62.62	79.34	57.82
	S.D.Dist.	34.83	31.08	33.69	30.41	33.83	28.10	30.73	25.69	24.34	30.72	31.84	30.26
	S.D.M.	3.76	4.01	4.24	3.61	4.33	3.27	4.14	3.16	2.79	3.84	1.73	1.65
	Diff.Means	29.76		12.48		15.04		29.36		20.64		21.52	
	C.R.	5.41		2.24		2.77		5.64		4.35		9.00	
	% Sup.	59.6		17.8		27.4		58.3		33.0		37.2	

Recall Gain—Non-Picture Items												
Mean	40.85	38.65	51.35	58.40	44.40	60.30	54.65	48.05	56.75	57.00	49.20	53.00
S.D.$_{Dist.}$	21.46	16.39	19.48	24.18	17.82	22.33	20.79	23.45	17.25	20.44	20.46	23.03
S.D.$_M$	2.31	2.12	2.45	2.86	2.28	2.60	2.80	2.89	1.98	2.56	1.11	1.26
Diff.$_{Means}$	2.20			7.05		15.90	6.60			.25		3.80
C.R.	.70			1.87		4.60	1.64			.08		2.26
% Sup.	5.7			13.7		35.8	13.7			0.4		7.7
Per Cent Retention of Final Test I on Recall Test												
Mean	73.46	69.56	67.70	72.65	67.67	75.65	65.60	82.64	71.69	76.43	69.86	66.62
S.D.$_{Dist.}$	16.11	17.85	15.18	17.25	16.74	18.09	16.32	17.52	12.00	17.07	15.39	18.09
S.D.$_M$	1.75	2.30	1.93	2.05	2.14	2.10	2.20	2.16	1.39	2.13	.84	.99
Diff.$_{Means}$	3.90			4.95		7.98		17.04		4.74	3.24	
C.R.	1.35			1.76		2.66		5.53		1.87	2.49	
% Sup.	5.6			7.3		3.9		26.0		6.6	4.9	

TABLE F
TOTAL SCIENCE TEST—EQUATED GROUP

FINAL TEST		A Exp.	A Cont.	B Exp.	B Cont.	C Exp.	C Cont.	D Exp.	D Cont.	E Exp.	E Cont.	Combined Cities Exp.	Combined Cities Cont.
	No. of Cases	88	66	68	82	63	79	44	70	78	70	341	367
Chronological Ages (in Months)	Mean	129.06	131.47	132.40	132.77	128.46	129.33	130.83	130.89	127.92	127.62	130.38	131.40
	S.D.$_{\text{Dist}}$	10.42	9.20	10.92	11.30	10.54	10.45	8.30	8.40	7.57	6.81	10.20	9.74
	S.D.M.	1.11	1.12	1.32	1.25	1.33	1.18	1.35	1.04	.86	.81	.56	.51
	Diff.$_{\text{Means}}$		2.41		.37		.87		.06	.30			1.02
	C.R.		1.53		.20		.49		.04	.25			1.34
	% Sup.		1.9		0.3		0.7		0.0	0.2			0.8
Intelligence Quotient	Mean	103.10	103.10	101.22	102.26	104.30	105.58	95.86	94.22	111.74	111.86	103.62	103.54
	S.D.$_{\text{Dist}}$	11.48	18.12	11.97	15.52	14.90	18.34	11.36	10.81	12.36	11.96	14.43	16.37
	S.D.M.	1.22	2.20	1.45	1.71	1.88	2.06	1.84	1.34	1.40	1.43	.79	.86
	Diff.$_{\text{Means}}$	0	0		1.04		1.28	1.64			.12	.08	
	C.R.	0.00	0.00		.46		.46	.72			.06	.07	
	% Sup.	0	0		1.0		1.2	1.7			0.1	0.1	
Initial Test	Mean	88.15	87.25	100.15	102.15	98.50	108.90	82.30	80.80	113.70	115.35	97.55	100.65
	S.D.$_{\text{Dist}}$	22.53	25.62	22.49	24.30	23.18	27.99	24.77	21.41	30.70	23.56	27.21	26.92
	S.D.M.	2.40	3.15	2.73	2.68	2.92	3.15	3.76	2.56	3.48	2.82	1.47	1.41
	Diff.$_{\text{Means}}$	.90			2.00		10.40	1.50			1.65		3.10
	C.R.	.23			.52		2.42	.33			.36		1.52
	% Sup.	1.0			2.0		10.6	1.9			1.5		3.2

Complete Final Test												
Mean	435.50	388.70	516.89	495.50	464.00	463.10	467.60	344.60	548.00	487.10	496.80	438.95
S.D.Dist.	123.75	107.27	94.97	109.85	111.65	118.64	83.75	78.84	77.87	68.84	110.70	115.38
S.D.M.	13.19	13.20	11.52	12.13	14.07	13.35	12.63	9.42	8.82	8.23	5.99	6.02
Diff.Means	46.80		21.39		.90		123.00		60.90		57.85	
C.R.	2.51		1.28		.05		7.80		5.05		6.81	
% Sup.	12.0		4.3		0.2		35.7		12.5		13.2	
Gain—Final Test over Initial Test												
Mean	154.98	124.10	193.46	177.38	168.82	146.34	191.78	108.58	191.46	150.66	178.26	142.90
S.D.Dist.	57.73	49.10	46.27	54.29	56.30	52.33	45.18	36.79	37.15	42.30	52.26	53.38
S.D.M.	6.15	6.04	5.61	6.00	7.09	5.89	6.81	4.40	4.21	5.06	2.83	2.79
Diff.Means	30.88		16.08		22.48		83.20		40.80		35.36	
C.R.	3.58		1.96		2.44		10.26		6.20		8.91	
% Sup.	24.9		9.1		15.4		76.6		27.1		24.7	

TABLE G

THE STRING CHOIR

FINAL TEST		A Exp.	A Cont.	B Exp.	B Cont.	C Exp.	C Cont.	D Exp.	D Cont.	E Exp.	E Cont.	COMBINED CITIES Exp.	COMBINED CITIES Cont.
	No. of Cases	93	92	33	23	100	121	126	123	110	147	462	506
Initial Test	Med.	47.25	48.06	28.18	39.50	40.50	41.28	26.10	29.72	37.61	39.28	36.05	39.90
	Mean	48.44	47.16	31.12	40.02	41.68	42.30	27.70	31.90	39.06	42.42	37.90	40.58
	Q.	8.09	9.10	7.04	9.50	8.67	9.11	4.79	8.38	6.84	5.82	9.55	9.22
	S.D.Dist.	11.64	12.69	9.46	12.87	12.63	12.31	8.44	11.75	9.84	11.17	12.82	13.08
	S.D.M.	1.21	1.32	1.65	2.68	1.26	1.12	.75	1.06	.94	.92	.60	.58
	Diff.Means	1.28			8.90		.62		4.20		3.36		2.68
	C.R.	.72			2.76		.37		3.23		2.55		3.23
	% Sup.	2.7			28.6		1.5		15.2		8.6		7.1
Complete Final Test	Med.	135.25	141.00	153.00	127.00	142.95	131.29	124.00	121.33	134.77	109.57	135.79	124.81
	Mean	132.31	136.42	149.44	125.44	140.17	129.70	117.22	119.56	135.49	112.39	134.98	123.25
	Q.	15.40	14.63	14.28	15.56	11.82	18.31	20.10	14.51	10.71	21.13	14.85	18.18
	S.D.Dist.	22.29	23.07	16.68	24.26	22.40	24.30	29.82	20.28	17.37	25.04	25.48	25.01
	S.D.M.	2.31	2.40	2.90	5.06	2.24	2.21	2.66	1.83	1.66	2.07	1.19	1.11
	Diff.Means		4.11	24.00		10.47			2.34	23.10		11.73	
	C.R.		1.23	4.12		3.32			.72	8.72		7.20	
	% Sup.		3.1	19.1		8.1			2.0	20.6		9.5	
Complete Final Test— Picture-Unit Items	Mean	100.45	100.09	110.83	87.73	103.81	92.08	88.63	85.66	99.91	78.88	98.56	87.82
	S.D.Dist.	16.96	16.83	12.29	17.60	16.77	19.54	22.16	16.15	13.20	18.12	18.73	19.11
	S.D.M.	1.76	1.75	2.14	3.67	1.68	1.78	1.97	1.31	1.26	1.49	.87	.83

Group	Stat	1	2	3	4	5	6	7	8	9	10	11	12
	Diff.Means	.36		23.10		11.73		2.97		21.03		10.74	
	C.R.	.15		5.44		4.79		1.25		10.78		8.95	
	% Sup.	0.4		26.3		12.7		3.5		26.7		12.2	
Complete Final Test—Non-Picture Items	Mean	31.75	36.34	38.56	37.27	36.40	37.27	28.54	33.67	35.50	33.43	33.25	35.02
	S.D.Dist.	8.59	9.14	6.70	8.32	9.10	7.64	10.03	7.34	7.36	8.81	9.41	8.41
	S.D.M.	.89	.95	1.17	1.73	.91	.69	.89	.59	.70	.73	.44	.36
	Diff.Means		4.59	1.29			.87		5.13	2.07			1.77
	C.R.		3.53	.62			.76		4.79	2.05			3.11
	% Sup.		14.5	3.5			2.4		18.0	6.2			5.3
Gain—Final Test over Initial Test	Med.	19.63	23.00	47.84	23.17	32.17	23.31	34.25	30.80	32.17	18.94	31.42	23.56
	Mean	20.32	23.52	48.38	24.58	31.30	24.12	34.04	30.02	32.20	18.18	31.28	23.72
	Q.	6.63	8.67	6.96	7.20	8.69	7.24	9.62	6.48	6.40	7.89	9.29	6.32
	S.D.Dist.	10.30	14.68	10.24	9.77	12.62	9.86	13.74	11.34	9.50	11.44	13.52	12.49
	S.D.M.	1.07	1.53	1.78	2.04	1.26	.90	1.22	1.02	.91	.94	.63	.56
	Diff.Means		3.20	23.80		8.86		3.45		13.23		7.56	
	C.R.		1.71	8.78		4.63		3.24		10.70		9.00	
	% Sup.		15.7	96.8		38.0		11.2		69.9		31.9	
Gain—Picture-Unit Items	Mean	16.30	17.80	36.90	15.68	24.12	17.40	26.76	22.04	24.42	12.34	24.24	17.06
	S.D.Dist.	8.08	10.49	8.44	7.06	10.20	7.77	10.67	9.48	7.78	8.81	10.62	9.66
	S.D.M.	.84	1.09	1.47	1.47	1.02	.71	.95	.85	.74	.73	.49	.43
	Diff.Means		1.50	21.22		6.72		4.72		12.08		7.18	
	C.R.		1.09	10.22		5.42		3.72		11.62		11.05	
	% Sup.		9.2	135.3		38.6		21.4		97.9		42.1	
Gain—Non-Picture Items	Mean	3.96	6.04	11.56	8.28	6.94	6.94	7.16	7.98	7.80	5.78	6.94	6.76
	S.D.Dist.	4.86	6.49	4.50	4.52	5.73	4.99	6.20	5.38	5.09	5.66	5.76	5.61
	S.D.M.	.50	.68	.78	.94	.57	.45	.55	.49	.49	.47	.27	.25
	Diff.Means		2.08	3.28		0	0		.82	2.02		.18	
	C.R.		2.48	2.69		0	0		1.11	2.97		.49	
	% Sup.		52.5	39.6		0	0		11.5	34.9		2.7	

TABLE G (Concluded)

RECALL TEST		A Exp.	A Cont.	B Exp.	B Cont.	C Exp.	C Cont.	D Exp.	D Cont.	E Exp.	E Cont.	COMBINED CITIES Exp.	COMBINED CITIES Cont.
No. of Cases		83	85	27	20	94	115	117	116	70	138	391	474
Recall Test Scores	Med.	67.00	69.50	84.00	61.00	72.00	64.85	57.90	60.50	68.28	61.61	67.89	62.97
	Mean	65.38	68.66	83.64	60.80	72.30	64.82	57.44	58.52	68.44	61.20	66.48	62.74
	Q.	8.98	8.54	6.37	6.00	8.50	7.16	11.25	8.00	7.59	9.86	9.52	8.62
	S.D.Dist.	12.44	13.02	7.56	13.02	11.90	11.22	14.02	11.85	10.80	12.60	14.29	12.70
	S.D.M.	1.37		1.45	2.91	1.23	1.05	1.30	1.10	1.29	1.07	.72	.58
	Diff.Means		3.28	22.84		7.48			1.08	7.24		3.74	
	C.R.		1.66	2.22		4.62			.64	4.31		4.07	
	% Sup.		5.0	37.6		11.5			1.9	11.8		6.0	
Recall Test Gain	Med.	17.00	20.12	50.50	18.50	30.50	22.23	29.79	28.17	30.25	17.77	28.33	21.93
	Mean	17.50	20.80	52.46	20.80	30.52	22.28	29.50	26.68	29.82	18.90	28.84	22.04
	Q.	6.90	8.20	8.00	4.66	8.37	6.55	9.98	8.60	6.35	8.43	10.12	8.36
	S.D.Dist.	9.98	14.36	10.40	8.84	11.78	9.42	13.74	12.11	10.02	11.56	14.26	12.06
	S.D.M.	1.10	1.56	2.00	1.98	1.22	.88	1.27	1.12	1.20	.98	.72	.55
	Diff.Means		3.30	31.66		8.24		2.82		10.92		6.80	
	C.R.		1.73	17.49		5.49		1.67		7.05		7.47	
	% Sup.		18.9	152.2		37.0		10.6		57.8		30.9	
Recall Gain— Picture-Unit Items	Mean	14.16	15.34	37.32	14.30	22.98	15.90	23.22	20.04	23.30	13.18	21.76	15.96
	S.D.Dist.	7.94	9.94	8.30	5.86	9.06	8.30	10.24	9.88	8.42	8.96	11.40	9.44
	S.D.M.	.87	1.08	1.60	1.31	.93	.77	.95	.92	1.01	.76	.58	.43
	Diff.Means		1.18	23.02		7.08		3.18		10.12		5.80	
	C.R.		.85	11.12		5.85		2.41		7.97		8.06	
	% Sup.		8.3	161.0		44.5		15.9		76.8		36.3	
Recall Gain— Non-Picture Items	Mean	3.35	5.42	15.22	7.15	7.57	6.40	6.17	6.73	6.64	5.64	6.43	6.12
	S.D.Dist.	5.20	6.83	4.09	5.15	6.01	4.59	6.27	6.12	5.04	5.52	6.38	5.73
	S.D.M.	.57	.74	.79	1.15	.62	.43	.58	.57	.60	.47	.32	.26
	Diff.Means		2.07	8.07		1.17			.56	1.00		.31	
	C.R.		2.23	5.76		1.56			.69	1.20		.77	
	% Sup.		61.8	112.9		18.3			9.1	17.7		5.0	

TABLE H
THE WOODWIND CHOIR

FINAL TEST		A Exp.	A Cont.	B Exp.	B Cont.	C Exp.	C Cont.	D Exp.	D Cont.	E Exp.	E Cont.	Combined Cities Exp.	Combined Cities Cont.
No. of Cases		90	93	30	23	102	110	137	127	107	148	466	501
Initial Test	Med.	35.36	32.38	22.50	24.00	29.00	35.74	11.22	17.72	21.20	29.58	22.50	27.18
	Mean	37.34	32.76	24.70	25.24	29.82	36.00	14.24	18.64	24.02	29.76	25.38	27.16
	Q.	8.40	7.77	6.66	5.84	9.61	9.80	3.68	6.04	7.80	7.56	10.16	8.89
	S.D.Dist.	12.44	11.14	11.85	8.87	12.33	14.68	7.48	9.70	12.18	10.61	13.96	13.13
	S.D.M.	1.31	1.16	2.16	1.85	1.22	1.40	.64	.86	1.18	.87	.65	.59
	Diff.Means	4.58			.54		6.18		4.40		5.74		1.78
	C.R.	2.62			.19		3.32		4.11		3.90		2.02
	% Sup.	14.0			2.2		20.7		30.9		23.9		7.0
Complete Final Test	Med.	95.50	94.00	117.70	80.00	107.50	101.50	86.26	89.71	95.95	87.10	97.39	91.87
	Mean	96.07	91.87	117.70	81.88	107.47	98.45	85.15	89.38	93.79	84.70	96.22	90.22
	Q.	14.92	13.96	11.07	10.31	15.12	13.88	19.50	11.45	10.41	15.54	16.08	14.22
	S.D.Dist.	19.23	20.65	20.13	17.35	20.94	20.32	24.25	18.58	16.71	21.44	22.93	20.88
	S.D.M.	2.03	2.14	3.67	3.62	2.07	1.94	2.07	1.65	1.62	1.76	1.06	.93
	Diff.Means	4.20		35.82		9.02			4.23	9.09		6.00	
	C.R.	1.42		6.96		3.18			1.60	3.80		4.26	
	% Sup.	4.6		43.7		9.2			5.0	10.7		6.7	
Complete Final Test—Picture—Unit Items	Mean	81.50	68.00	90.15	59.85	80.25	73.50	64.30	66.50	70.95	61.10	72.35	66.40
	S.D.Dist.	16.50	16.43	17.72	13.78	17.37	16.79	20.10	14.81	13.84	17.40	18.91	17.00
	S.D.M.	1.74	1.70	3.23	2.87	1.72	1.60	1.72	1.31	1.34	1.43	.88	.76
	Diff.Means	13.50		30.30		6.75			2.20	9.85		5.95	
	C.R.	5.56		7.01		2.87			1.02	5.03		5.13	
	% Sup.	19.9		50.6		9.2			3.4	16.1		9.0	

TABLE H (Concluded)

FINAL TEST		A Exp.	A Cont.	B Exp.	B Cont.	C Exp.	C Cont.	D Exp.	D Cont.	E Exp.	E Cont.	Combined Exp.	Combined Cont.
No. of Cases		90	93	30	23	102	110	137	127	107	148	466	501
Complete Final Test—Non-Picture Items	Mean	24.50	24.00	27.44	21.90	27.38	25.84	20.78	22.94	22.72	23.56	23.82	23.90
	S.D.Dist.	4.83	5.55	4.45	5.20	4.97	5.38	5.73	5.81	5.00	5.98	5.76	5.84
	S.D.M.	.51	.58	.81	1.08	.49	.51	.49	.52	.48	.49	.27	.26
	Diff.Means	.50		5.54		1.54			2.16		.84		.08
	C.R.	.63		4.10		2.17			3.04		1.22		.22
	% Sup.	2.1		25.3		6.0			10.4		3.7		0.3
Gain—Final Test Over Initial Test	Med.	25.50	26.75	51.50	38.00	41.50	29.50	44.72	39.38	38.22	27.05	38.34	31.02
	Mean	26.22	25.74	52.50	34.16	41.40	30.02	43.94	39.28	36.85	27.68	38.86	31.08
	Q.	7.33	9.08	11.00	9.10	9.82	9.19	12.42	10.45	10.61	11.32	11.10	10.34
	S.D.Dist.	10.57	12.14	13.85	11.59	13.07	12.13	15.62	14.58	14.46	15.08	15.65	14.61
	S.D.M.	1.11	1.26	2.53	2.42	1.29	1.16	1.33	1.29	1.40	1.24	.73	.65
	Diff.Means	.48		18.34		11.38		4.66		9.17		7.78	
	C.R.	.29		5.23		6.58		2.52		4.90		7.94	
	% Sup.	1.9		53.7		37.9		11.9		33.1		25.0	
Gain—Picture-Unit Items	Mean	16.18	15.01	36.61	21.10	27.49	18.82	29.26	25.06	23.50	16.66	25.51	19.15
	S.D.Dist.	8.64	9.35	11.28	31.61	10.71	8.43	12.81	11.30	11.27	12.00	12.44	11.16
	S.D.M.	.91	.97	2.06	6.59	1.06	.80	1.09	1.00	1.09	.99	.58	.50
	Diff.Means	1.17		15.51		8.67		4.20		6.84		6.36	
	C.R.	.88		2.25		6.47		2.84		4.65		8.26	
	% Sup.	7.8		73.5		46.1		16.8		41.1		33.2	
Gain—Non-Picture Items	Mean	10.07	10.87	16.07	13.13	13.82	11.14	14.96	13.97	13.36	11.16	13.47	11.90
	S.D.Dist.	4.83	5.48	5.15	5.10	5.48	6.31	5.35	5.64	5.47	5.35	5.61	5.82
	S.D.M.	.51	.57	.94	1.06	.54	.60	.46	.50	.53	.44	.26	.26

Recall Test		82	87	26	21	96	105	126	120	65	142	395	475
No. of Cases	Diff.Means		.80	2.94		2.68		.99		2.20		1.57	
	C.R.		1.05	2.07		3.31		1.46		3.19		4.24	
	% Sup.		7.9	22.4		24.1		7.1		19.7		13.2	
Recall Test Scores	Med.	54.30	58.67	72.50	51.00	62.05	62.00	47.25	53.50	61.00	53.70	57.31	56.04
	Mean	55.14	58.29	73.05	50.28	61.05	60.15	48.27	50.85	59.49	52.95	56.28	54.87
	Q.	11.50	9.39	13.50	15.93	10.37	10.58	9.15	11.00	7.27	12.60	11.36	11.16
	S.D.Dist.	16.35	16.18	14.97	17.10	14.86	15.42	17.31	15.29	11.73	16.47	16.98	16.38
	S.D.M.	1.81	1.73	2.94	3.73	1.52	1.50	1.54	1.40	1.45	1.38	.85	.75
	Diff.Means		3.15	22.77		.90			2.58	6.54		1.41	
	C.R.		1.26	4.79		.42			1.24	3.27		1.25	
	% Sup.		5.7	45.3		1.5			5.3	12.4		2.6	
Recall Test Gain (Recall Minus Initial Test)	Med.	20.88	25.75	46.00	25.00	31.25	23.00	35.70	34.00	36.62	23.71	32.65	26.37
	Mean	20.89	25.39	47.38	24.43	30.91	23.74	34.78	32.14	35.74	23.38	31.96	26.08
	Q.	11.79	7.65	8.37	11.44	9.94	9.74	10.31	10.65	9.18	10.27	11.24	10.48
	S.D.Dist.	14.19	13.52	14.10	13.47	13.85	14.38	15.66	15.48	14.58	15.09	16.11	15.14
	S.D.M.	1.57	1.45	2.77	2.94	1.41	1.40	1.40	1.41	1.81	1.27	.81	.69
	Diff.Means		4.50	22.95		7.17		2.64		12.36		5.88	
	C.R.		2.10	5.68		3.60		1.33		5.59		5.55	
	% Sup.		21.6	93.9		30.2		8.2		52.9		22.5	
Recall Gain—Picture-Unit Items	Mean	14.64	16.84	33.42	16.22	22.08	16.70	24.36	21.96	24.56	15.00	22.42	17.52
	S.D.Dist.	12.47	10.00	11.52	8.68	10.38	11.10	11.97	10.85	11.72	11.07	12.56	10.80
	S.D.M.	1.38	1.07	2.26	1.89	1.06	1.08	1.07	.99	1.45	.93	.63	.50
	Diff.Means		2.20	17.20		5.38		2.40		9.56		4.90	
	C.R.		1.26	2.95		3.56		1.64		5.56		6.12	
	% Sup.		15.0	106.0		32.2		10.9		63.7		27.9	
Recall Gain—Non-Picture Items	Mean	6.44	8.32	14.12	8.10	9.31	7.19	10.41	10.23	11.06	8.29	9.67	8.53
	S.D.Dist.	7.41	5.89	5.10	6.17	5.95	5.93	5.52	6.55	4.97	5.84	5.87	6.17
	S.D.M.	.82	.63	1.00	1.35	.61	.58	.49	.60	.62	.49	.30	.28
	Diff.Means		1.88	6.02		2.12		.18		2.77		1.14	
	C.R.		1.81	5.10		2.49		.23		3.51		2.78	
	% Sup.		29.2	74.3		29.5		1.8		33.4		13.4	

TABLE I
THE BRASS CHOIR

Final Test		No. of Cases	A Exp.	A Cont.	B Exp.	B Cont.	C Exp.	C Cont.	D Exp.	D Cont.	E Exp.	E Cont.	Combined Cities Exp.	Combined Cities Cont.
			89	83	29	23	101	123	175	120	199	228	593	577
Initial Test	Med.		36.30	28.64	33.50	35.00	32.80	31.50	20.72	22.50	22.54	24.63	24.70	27.26
	Mean		35.94	30.76	33.44	34.20	33.24	33.46	22.36	23.86	22.72	28.08	26.92	28.98
	Q.		9.21	5.35	6.32	5.65	8.37	7.94	4.95	6.57	5.12	10.60	7.65	8.54
	S.D.Dist.		11.90	9.41	8.62	8.43	11.77	10.80	9.39	10.10	8.02	13.39	11.36	11.98
	S.D.M.		1.26	1.03	1.60	1.76	1.17	.97	.71	.92	.57	.88	.47	.50
	Diff.Means		5.18			.76		.22		1.50		5.36		2.06
	C.R.		3.18			.32		.14		1.29		5.10		2.99
	% Sup.		16.8			2.3		0.7		6.7		23.6		7.7
Complete Final Test	Med.		130.20	107.70	155.15	121.13	133.65	117.80	124.60	114.15	94.85	98.70	121.20	108.75
	Mean		125.85	105.35	155.75	114.95	130.55	115.30	118.55	113.85	95.80	99.55	115.90	107.30
	Q.		14.80	18.00	8.35	14.21	17.15	15.65	17.10	18.75	22.10	17.13	22.20	18.37
	S.D.Dist.		24.25	26.65	12.45	20.16	23.62	24.25	28.01	23.73	30.65	25.48	31.62	25.90
	S.D.M.		2.57	2.93	2.31	4.20	2.35	2.19	2.12	2.17	2.17	1.69	1.30	1.08
	Diff.Means		20.50		40.80		15.25		4.70			3.75	8.60	
	C.R.		5.26		8.52		4.75		1.55			1.36	5.09	
	% Sup.		19.5		35.5		13.2		4.1			3.9	8.0	
Complete Final Test—Picture-Unit Items	Mean		111.18	91.50	134.82	96.18	113.26	101.02	105.06	100.94	86.26	87.06	102.54	93.90
	S.D.Dist.		21.19	22.96	9.07	16.57	18.78	21.03	24.88	21.33	26.98	21.98	26.97	22.59
	S.D.M.		2.25	2.52	1.68	3.45	1.87	1.90	1.88	1.95	1.91	1.46	1.11	.94

Complete Final Test— Non-Picture Items												
Diff.Means	19.68		38.64		12.24		4.12			.80	8.64	
C.R.	5.82		10.06		4.58		1.52			.33	5.96	
% Sup.	21.5		40.2		12.1		4.1			0.9	9.2	
Mean	14.99	14.40	21.10	18.61	17.28	14.12	13.43	12.99	9.93	12.53	13.52	13.46
S.D.Dist.	5.08	5.55	4.77	5.43	6.28	5.11	5.44	4.73	5.40	5.19	6.31	5.25
S.D.M.	.54	.61	.89	1.13	.62	.46	.41	.43	.38	.34	.26	.22
Diff.Means	.59		2.49		3.16		.44			2.60	.06	
C.R.	.73		1.73		4.10		.75			5.10	.18	
% Sup.	4.1		13.4		22.4		3.4			26.2	0.4	
Gain— Final Test Over Initial Test												
Med.	31.70	26.88	58.10	28.50	39.16	31.12	42.72	38.66	30.72	27.26	37.86	31.04
Mean	33.10	28.30	58.02	30.84	39.86	31.12	40.78	37.94	29.98	28.84	36.70	31.22
Q.	9.88	8.26	5.11	7.88	10.49	9.31	9.96	9.17	11.10	11.36	10.94	10.30
S.D.Dist.	14.21	13.59	9.92	9.33	15.22	13.44	15.00	14.43	15.54	16.83	16.34	15.38
S.D.M.	1.51	1.49	1.84	1.95	1.51	1.21	1.13	1.32	1.10	1.11	.67	.64
Diff.Means	4.80		27.18		8.74		2.84		1.14		5.48	
C.R.	2.26		10.14		4.53		1.63		.73		5.89	
% Sup.	17.0		88.1		28.1		7.5		4.0		17.6	
Gain— Picture-Unit Items												
Mean	26.92	23.98	45.16	22.00	32.59	26.77	36.43	33.97	27.34	23.59	31.72	26.41
S.D.Dist.	11.80	12.06	7.86	8.39	12.12	11.10	13.92	13.41	13.57	14.97	13.92	13.89
S.D.M.	1.25	1.32	1.46	1.75	1.21	1.00	1.05	1.22	.96	.99	.57	.58
Diff.Means	2.94		23.16		5.82		2.46		3.75		5.31	
C.R.	1.62		10.16		3.71		1.53		2.72		6.56	
% Sup.	12.3		105.3		21.7		7.2		15.9		20.1	
Gain— Non-Picture Items												
Mean	6.22	4.18	12.66	8.87	7.27	4.29	4.29	3.94	2.61	5.34	4.93	4.80
S.D.Dist.	5.05	3.80	4.10	3.97	5.54	4.47	4.04	3.97	4.29	4.53	5.20	4.41
S.D.M.	.54	.42	.76	.83	.55	.40	.31	.36	.30	.30	.21	.18
Diff.Means	2.04		3.79		2.98		.35			2.73	.13	
C.R.	3.00		3.35		4.38		.73			6.50	.46	
% Sup.	48.8		42.7		69.5		8.9			104.6	2.7	

TABLE I (*Concluded*)

RECALL TEST		A Exp.	A Cont.	B Exp.	B Cont.	C Exp.	C Cont.	D Exp.	D Cont.	E Exp.	E Cont.	COMBINED CITIES Exp.	COMBINED CITIES Cont.
No. of Cases		79	78	26	22	98	117	126	116	128	213	457	546
Recall Test Scores	Med.	61.00	54.50	77.50	60.50	62.75	57.00	49.79	54.93	52.10	54.00	56.88	55.04
	Mean	61.10	52.55	78.38	57.08	62.66	58.01	50.06	54.23	52.70	54.62	57.02	55.07
	Q.	12.54	11.81	11.81	7.69	12.63	10.79	12.37	11.27	13.85	10.04	13.81	10.76
	S.D.Dist.	15.96	15.89	13.53	14.46	17.22	14.01	16.47	15.34	17.46	14.13	18.24	14.73
	S.D.M.	1.80	1.80	2.65	3.08	1.74	1.30	1.47	1.42	1.54	.97	.85	.63
	Diff.Means	8.55		21.30		4.65			4.17		1.92	1.95	
	C.R.	3.35		5.25		2.14			2.04		1.05	1.84	
	% Sup.	16.3		37.3		8.1			8.3		3.6	3.5	
Recall Test Gain	Med.	24.65	23.00	45.50	21.50	27.77	22.88	29.90	29.75	28.70	26.16	28.62	25.41
	Mean	24.98	21.47	45.38	23.27	29.96	24.17	29.51	30.50	29.33	26.60	29.69	26.03
	Q.	9.31	12.85	9.06	7.20	7.53	9.41	11.87	10.50	11.29	11.69	10.23	10.40
	S.D.Dist.	13.95	16.09	12.57	11.55	13.86	12.14	16.29	14.59	15.24	16.50	15.45	15.34
	S.D.M.	1.57	1.82	2.47	2.46	1.40	1.12	1.45	1.35	1.35	1.13	.72	.66
	Diff.Means	3.51		22.11		5.79			.99	2.73		3.66	
	C.R.	1.46		6.34		3.23			.50	1.55		3.73	
	% Sup.	16.3		95.0		23.1			3.4	10.3		14.1	
Recall Gain—Picture-Unit Items	Mean	20.40	17.80	36.04	17.40	25.16	20.08	25.62	26.46	24.96	22.08	25.02	21.78
	S.D.Dist.	11.86	14.18	13.88	10.82	12.01	10.89	15.06	12.85	12.78	14.20	13.53	13.46
	S.D.M.	1.33	1.61	2.72	2.31	1.21	1.01	1.34	1.19	1.13	.97	.63	.58
	Diff.Means	2.60		18.64		5.08			.84	2.88		3.24	
	C.R.	1.24		5.22		3.22			.47	1.93		3.76	
	% Sup.	14.6		107.1		25.3			3.3	13.0		14.9	
Recall Gain—Non-Picture Items	Mean	4.75	3.72	8.96	5.86	4.65	4.09	3.88	4.09	4.05	4.50	4.56	4.30
	S.D.Dist.	3.98	4.06	4.01	3.96	4.68	3.68	3.50	3.28	4.11	4.20	4.20	4.01
	S.D.M.	.45	.46	.79	.85	.47	.34	.31	.30	.36	.29	.20	.17
	Diff.Means	1.03		3.10	1.21	.56			.21		.45	.26	
	C.R.	1.61		2.67		.97			.49		.98	.74	
	% Sup.	27.7		52.9		13.7			5.4		11.1	6.0	

TABLE J
THE PERCUSSION GROUP

FINAL TEST	No. of Cases	A Exp.	A Cont.	B Exp.	B Cont.	C Exp.	C Cont.	D Exp.	D Cont.	E Exp.	E Cont.	Combined Exp.	Combined Cont.
		89	97	31	21	99	120	160	120	148	214	527	572
Initial Test	Med.	35.66	34.66	37.10	42.00	33.34	41.30	25.31	29.00	24.05	28.64	28.42	32.66
	Mean	37.18	36.88	38.20	42.26	34.76	41.24	27.62	32.64	27.26	30.34	31.10	34.66
	Q.	9.67	10.07	5.84	9.98	8.30	10.14	7.15	9.33	7.15	9.11	8.72	10.10
	S.D.Dist.	14.23	13.92	9.71	14.46	13.13	12.77	11.80	14.34	12.81	13.01	13.41	14.17
	S.D.M.	1.51	1.41	1.74	3.15	1.32	1.17	.93	1.31	1.05	.89	.58	.59
	Diff.Means	.30			4.06		6.48		5.02		3.08		3.56
	C.R.	.14			1.13		3.68		3.12		2.23		4.29
	% Sup.	0.8			10.6		18.6		18.2		11.3		11.4
Complete Final Test	Med.	169.65	134.25	213.00	150.00	180.10	165.50	158.35	131.50	138.22	115.50	159.87	132.77
	Mean	157.85	132.35	211.55	156.10	174.10	157.75	155.80	132.95	136.20	114.35	157.50	131.95
	Q.	24.32	24.27	13.44	18.06	25.90	24.65	24.79	23.75	28.12	29.87	28.57	29.37
	S.D.Dist.	36.70	33.78	19.64	32.38	36.56	34.26	32.51	35.62	37.95	38.79	39.65	39.79
	S.D.M.	3.89	3.43	3.53	7.06	3.67	3.13	2.57	3.25	3.12	2.05	1.73	1.66
	Diff.Means	25.50		55.45		16.35		22.85		21.85		25.55	
	C.R.	4.91		7.03		3.39		5.52		5.34		10.65	
	% Sup.	19.3		35.5		10.4		17.2		19.1		19.4	
Complete Final Test— Picture-Unit Items	Mean	123.20	99.20	157.65	111.05	126.65	117.65	120.50	96.25	102.15	84.90	119.15	97.55
	S.D.Dist.	29.47	25.70	13.05	23.80	28.49	25.50	25.14	26.25	28.03	30.05	30.05	30.00
	S.D.M.	3.12	2.61	2.34	5.19	2.86	2.33	1.99	2.40	2.30	2.05	1.31	1.25
	Diff.Means	24.00		46.60		9.00		24.25		17.25		21.60	
	C.R.	5.90		8.19		2.44		7.72		5.60		11.93	
	% Sup.	24.2		42.0		7.6		25.2		20.3		22.1	

TABLE J (*Concluded*)

FINAL TEST		A Exp.	A Cont.	B Exp.	B Cont.	C Exp.	C Cont.	D Exp.	D Cont.	E Exp.	E Cont.	COMBINED CITIES Exp.	COMBINED CITIES Cont.
No. of Cases		89	97	31	21	99	120	160	120	148	214	527	572
Complete Final Test—Non-Picture Items	Mean	40.70	37.44	54.54	44.92	46.24	40.10	35.58	36.60	34.44	29.38	40.24	35.08
	S.D.Dist.	11.82	11.76	9.14	10.82	12.18	10.84	10.34	11.44	11.66	10.88	12.68	12.10
	S.D.M.	1.25	1.19	1.64	2.36	1.22	.99	.82	1.04	.95	.74	.55	.51
	Diff.Means	3.26		9.62		6.14			1.02	6.06		5.16	
	C.R.	1.88		3.35		3.91			.77	5.05		6.88	
	% Sup.	8.7		21.4		15.3			2.9	20.6		14.7	
Gain—Final Test Over Initial Test	Med.	50.90	36.26	80.00	42.00	60.10	48.50	56.83	40.00	44.70	35.94	53.91	40.53
	Mean	47.56	37.16	79.72	44.88	59.00	47.80	55.94	40.00	43.64	34.62	53.60	40.06
	Q.	11.02	10.51	9.57	7.62	11.53	8.83	12.22	10.58	12.25	13.92	13.59	12.42
	S.D.Dist.	17.29	15.90	12.47	12.96	18.52	14.99	18.41	15.63	18.29	18.67	19.82	16.27
	S.D.M.	1.83	1.61	2.24	2.83	1.86	1.37	1.46	1.43	1.50	1.28	.87	.68
	Diff.Means	10.40		34.84		11.20		15.94		9.02		13.54	
	C.R.	4.26		9.65		4.85		7.81		4.58		12.31	
	% Sup.	28.0		77.6		23.4		39.9		26.1		33.8	
Gain—Picture-Unit Items	Mean	39.46	27.97	63.82	35.29	46.30	37.81	48.73	31.06	37.33	30.22	44.38	32.32
	S.D.Dist.	14.49	18.21	9.15	11.40	13.53	11.49	14.61	12.18	14.46	15.66	15.69	13.92
	S.D.M.	1.54	1.85	1.64	2.49	1.36	1.05	1.16	1.11	1.19	1.07	1.68	.58
	Diff.Means	11.49		28.53		8.49		17.67		9.11		12.06	
	C.R.	4.77		9.57		4.94		10.98		4.44		13.55	
	% Sup.	41.1		80.8		22.5		56.9		23.5		37.3	
Gain—Non-Picture Items	Mean	7.98	6.10	16.24	9.46	12.56	10.06	7.70	9.08	8.34	6.20	11.38	7.72
	S.D.Dist.	6.54	6.00	5.74	4.84	8.22	6.70	6.14	6.18	6.32	5.78	7.10	6.32
	S.D.M.	.69	.61	1.03	1.06	.83	.61	.49	.56	.52	.45	.31	.26

RECALL TEST	77	92	28	19	97	116	114	116	140	204	456	547
Diff.Means	1.88		6.78		2.50			1.38	2.14		3.66	
C.R.	2.04		4.58		2.43			1.86	3.24		9.15	
% Sup.	30.8		71.7		24.9			17.9	34.5		47.4	
No. of Cases	77	92	28	19	97	116	114	116	140	204	456	547
Recall Test Scores												
Med.	80.90	60.50	104.50	79.50	84.79	85.30	69.30	63.17	62.90	58.78	73.98	66.29
Mean	76.58	65.22	103.78	81.86	81.74	82.66	68.82	65.82	66.54	60.50	74.34	67.86
Q.	17.13	16.43	7.00	15.75	17.49	12.33	15.94	14.61	18.00	16.29	18.88	17.75
S.D.Dist.	23.92	22.32	13.56	20.60	18.11	19.60	21.52	22.04	23.24	22.96	24.57	23.58
S.D.M.	2.74	2.33	2.56	4.73	1.84	1.82	2.02	2.05	1.96	1.61	1.15	1.01
Diff.Means	11.35		21.92			.92	3.00		6.04		6.48	
C.R.	3.15		4.07			.36	1.04		2.38		4.24	
% Sup.	17.4		26.8			1.1	4.6		10.0		9.5	
Recall Test Gain												
Med.	42.00	25.50	63.00	39.75	48.00	43.50	43.93	34.50	37.07	28.93	43.88	33.22
Mean	39.78	27.81	64.59	39.33	46.95	41.19	43.68	33.45	39.27	29.94	43.65	33.03
Q.	14.83	13.10	6.25	9.75	13.10	10.75	14.40	11.25	14.15	12.74	14.14	13.38
S.D.Dist.	18.74	18.37	14.28	12.60	20.36	15.73	20.19	15.93	18.81	18.06	20.19	17.75
S.D.M.	2.14	1.92	2.70	2.89	2.07	1.46	1.89	1.48	1.59	1.26	.95	.76
Diff.Means	11.97		25.26		5.76		10.23		9.33		10.62	
C.R.	4.16		6.38		2.28		4.26		4.60		8.70	
% Sup.	43.0		64.2		14.0		30.6		31.2		32.2	
Recall Gain—Picture-Unit Items												
Mean	31.87	24.25	52.87	32.26	37.63	31.51	37.54	25.93	29.98	25.21	35.80	26.77
S.D.Dist.	15.53	15.27	11.05	11.33	15.53	12.71	16.62	13.15	17.06	14.94	16.32	14.40
S.D.M.	1.77	1.59	2.09	2.60	1.58	1.18	1.56	1.22	1.44	1.04	.76	.62
Diff.Means	7.62		20.61		6.12		11.61		4.77		9.03	
C.R.	3.22		6.17		3.11		5.86		2.68		9.21	
% Sup.	31.4		63.9		19.4		44.8		18.9		33.7	
Recall Gain—Non-Picture Items												
Mean	7.78	3.47	12.04	7.21	9.45	8.57	6.23	7.38	7.22	4.65	8.00	6.07
S.D.Dist.	5.96	6.58	6.76	4.23	7.35	6.76	6.38	5.26	6.80	6.15	6.85	6.44
S.D.M.	.68	.69	1.28	.97	.75	.63	.60	.49	.57	.43	.32	.28
Diff.Means	4.31		4.83		.88			1.15	2.57		1.93	
C.R.	4.44		3.00		.90			1.49	3.62		4.49	
% Sup.	124.2		66.1		10.3			18.5	55.3		31.8	

TABLE K

TOTAL MUSIC TEST

(Including City E, Chronological Ages and Intelligence)

FINAL TEST		A Exp.	A Cont.	B Exp.	B Cont.	C Exp.	C Cont.	D Exp.	D Cont.	E Exp.	E Cont.	COMBINED CITIES Exp.	COMBINED CITIES Cont.
No. of Cases		71	77	26	17	85	94	98	93	230	344	280	281
Chronological Ages (In Months)	Med.	153.72	152.70	157.50	151.20	152.46	152.22	151.96	151.67	153.18	152.94	153.12	152.57
	Mean	154.23	153.00	158.76	156.00	152.73	152.85	153.12	154.47	155.49	154.53	154.56	154.11
	Q.	4.77	5.46	6.50	4.30	6.30	4.72	5.14	6.78	6.39	5.86	5.89	5.73
	S.D.Dist.	9.22	8.50	10.57	12.09	9.67	8.03	8.22	12.05	10.99	10.56	10.11	10.34
	S.D.M.	1.09	.97	2.07	2.93	1.05	.84	.83	1.28	.73	.57	.45	.42
	Diff.Means	1.23		2.76		.12			1.35	.96		.45	
	C.R.	.84		.77		.09			.88	1.03		.73	
	% Sup.	0.8		1.8		0.1			0.9	0.6		0.3	
Intelligence Quotient	Med.	98.00	101.50	99.16	100.50	101.94	101.50	95.00	96.07	99.40	100.83	98.29	100.30
	Mean	98.96	101.44	100.26	101.02	101.36	102.82	94.66	98.20	100.82	102.64	99.42	101.84
	Q.	7.53	8.00	10.45	6.50	13.00	9.54	7.33	7.31	10.67	9.27	9.61	9.18
	S.D.Dist.	11.48	11.36	14.39	11.13	15.24	12.36	10.62	11.71	13.51	14.08	13.33	13.20
	S.D.M.	1.36	1.30	2.82	2.70	1.65	1.30	1.07	1.24	.90	.76	.59	.53
	Diff.Means		2.48		.76		1.46		3.54		1.82		2.42
	C.R.		1.32		.19		.70		2.16		1.54		3.06
	% Sup.		2.5		0.8		1.4		3.7		1.8		2.4

TABLE L
TOTAL MUSIC TEST

		CITIES								CITIES A–D COMBINED	
		A		B		C		D			
FINAL TEST	No. of Cases	Exp.	Cont.	Exp.	Cont.	Exp.	Cont.	Exp.	Cont.	Exp.	Cont.
		71	77	26	17	85	94	98	93	280	281
Initial Test	Med.	155.00	150.08	126.50	141.50	138.12	149.75	83.57	105.50	121.05	137.26
	Mean	156.14	147.86	125.12	136.58	140.78	152.84	89.54	108.86	125.30	135.92
	Q.	29.50	21.99	22.65	21.37	31.00	26.75	15.12	26.57	35.62	28.15
	S.D.Dist.	37.86	35.48	29.03	31.93	39.11	40.71	29.43	36.96	44.40	42.30
	S.D.M.	4.49	4.04	5.69	7.74	4.24	4.20	2.97	3.83	2.65	2.52
	Diff.Means	8.28			11.46		12.06		19.32		10.62
	C.R.	1.37			1.19		2.02		3.98		2.90
	% Sup.	5.6			9.2		8.6		21.6		8.5
Final Test I	Med.	290.50	268.83	366.83	272.50	316.50	288.16	273.50	255.16	290.11	270.04
(Items Equivalent to	Mean	285.61	264.51	363.04	269.96	310.81	284.90	265.08	252.46	293.34	271.42
Initial Test)	Q.	30.33	26.44	21.50	14.50	49.04	38.33	45.00	33.58	40.08	31.82
	S.D.Dist.	49.34	48.63	37.96	37.58	54.69	53.21	58.50	50.46	60.80	52.24
	S.D.M	5.86	5.54	7.45	9.12	5.93	5.49	5.91	5.23	3.63	3.12
	Diff.Means	21.10		93.07		25.91		12.62		21.92	
	C.R.	2.62		7.90		3.21		1.60		4.58	
	% Sup.	8.0		34.5		9.1		5.0		8.1	
Complete Final Test	Med.	534.50	477.14	632.50	474.50	558.90	507.16	483.70	460.50	536.03	477.12
	Mean	516.66	473.94	632.50	467.86	555.38	499.06	473.62	455.06	524.18	475.70
	Q.	58.80	48.00	35.36	33.64	56.66	77.66	70.85	58.47	69.17	57.76
	S.D.Dist.	89.22	83.81	56.82	61.41	84.58	94.13	102.13	82.70	102.08	87.84
	S.D.M.	10.59	9.55	11.14	14.89	9.17	9.71	10.32	8.58	6.10	5.24
	Diff.Means	42.72		164.64		56.32		18.56		48.40	
	C.R.	3.00		8.85		4.22		1.38		6.03	
	% Sup.	9.0		35.2		11.3		4.1		10.2	

TABLE L (Continued)

FINAL TEST	No. of Cases	CITIES A — Exp.	A — Cont.	B — Exp.	B — Cont.	C — Exp.	C — Cont.	D — Exp.	D — Cont.	CITIES A–D COMBINED — Exp.	Combined — Cont.
	No. of Cases	71	77	26	17	85	94	98	93	280	281
Complete Final Test Picture-Unit Items	Mean	403.00	360.10	486.80	346.30	424.90	381.50	376.40	349.30	408.10	363.90
	S.D.Dist.	67.49	64.53	41.46	44.02	63.76	73.39	79.64	63.92	76.10	66.60
	S.D.M.	8.01	7.35	8.13	10.68	6.92	7.57	8.05	6.63	4.55	3.97
	Diff.Means	42.90		140.50		43.40		27.10		44.20	
	C.R.	3.95		10.47		4.23		2.60		7.32	
	% Sup.	11.9		40.6		11.4		7.8		12.1	
Complete Final Test Non-Picture Items	Mean	113.97	113.52	140.76	120.87	128.79	117.39	97.11	105.36	115.17	112.56
	S.D.Dist.	24.41	22.64	17.55	18.91	25.05	22.78	25.38	22.26	28.77	23.01
	S.D.M.	2.90	2.58	3.44	4.59	2.72	2.35	2.56	2.35	1.72	1.37
	Diff.Means	.45		19.89		11.40			8.25	2.61	
	C.R.	.12		3.47		3.18			2.39	1.17	
	% Sup.	0.4		16.5		9.7			8.5	2.3	
Gain—Final Test I over Initial Test	Med.	132.07	116.30	240.50	124.70	172.25	133.70	180.50	144.12	162.50	132.36
	Mean	128.30	115.94	237.26	133.04	172.64	132.68	174.62	141.80	167.48	131.96
	Q.	19.38	23.69	21.25	17.25	25.00	17.95	36.57	24.92	35.00	23.25
	S.D.Dist.	33.12	36.41	32.90	21.67	41.09	29.19	48.86	39.77	50.16	36.96
	S.D.M.	3.93	4.15	6.45	5.25	4.46	3.01	4.94	4.12	3.00	2.21
	Diff.Means	12.36		104.22		39.96		32.82		35.52	
	C.R.	2.16		12.53		7.43		1.41		9.52	
	% Sup.	10.7		78.3		30.1		23.1		26.9	

Gain—Picture-Unit Items										
Mean	99.98	131.30	109.94	141.20	99.62	130.52	94.40	182.78	89.72	99.74
S.D.Dist.	29.70	39.36	34.08	38.52	20.94	29.82	22.26	23.70	30.60	26.28
S.D.M.	1.77	2.35	3.53	3.89	2.16	3.23	5.40	4.65	3.49	3.12
Diff.Means		31.32		31.26		30.90		88.38		10.02
C.R.		10.65		5.95		7.94		12.40		2.14
% Sup.		31.3		28.4		31.0		93.6		11.2
Gain—Non-Picture Items										
Mean	32.46	37.34	34.30	34.56	32.18	41.72	40.38	56.04	28.82	28.30
S.D.Dist.	12.84	16.14	12.26	13.46	12.06	17.02	11.20	11.74	13.70	12.04
S.D.M.	.77	.97	1.27	1.36	1.24	1.85	2.72	2.30	1.56	1.43
Diff.Means		4.88		.26		9.54		15.66	.52	
C.R.		3.94		.14		4.28		4.40	.25	
% Sup.		15.0		0.8		29.6		38.8	1.8	
Recall Test										
No. of Cases	269	263	90	92	91	84	16	23	72	64
Recall Test Scores										
Med.	249.50	265.42	232.50	227.50	266.21	285.83	244.50	350.50	249.50	269.83
Mean	247.70	259.94	232.50	224.50	263.94	280.42	244.50	339.14	246.82	255.62
Q.	37.59	46.43	35.66	43.20	37.05	36.80	34.00	35.00	35.34	44.00
S.D.Dist.	55.76	67.36	55.04	60.56	52.02	58.68	47.36	42.08	57.34	60.02
S.D.M.	3.40	4.15	5.80	6.31	5.45	6.40	11.84	8.77	6.76	7.50
Diff.Means		12.24	8.00			16.48		94.64		8.80
C.R.		2.28	.93			1.96		6.42		.87
% Sup.		4.9	3.6			6.2		38.7		3.6
Recall Test Gain (Recall Minus Initial Test)										
Med.	109.10	134.85	120.50	138.50	107.61	141.83	114.10	212.50	93.30	112.50
Mean	110.02	134.02	122.58	134.74	108.50	139.78	108.98	209.70	97.50	104.50
Q.	24.99	34.83	29.39	34.40	20.20	26.66	16.00	27.50	25.34	28.00
S.D.Dist.	42.80	52.48	45.20	52.88	30.90	43.22	26.32	33.68	50.45	41.52
S.D.M.	2.61	3.24	4.76	5.51	3.24	4.72	6.58	7.02	5.94	5.19
Diff.Means		24.00		12.16		31.28		100.72		7.00
C.R.		5.77		1.67		5.46		10.47		.89
% Sup.		21.8		9.9		28.8		92.4		7.2

TABLE L (*Concluded*)

		CITIES								CITIES A–D COMBINED	
		A		B		C		D			
RECALL TEST		Exp.	Cont.	Exp.	Cont.	Exp.	Cont.	Exp.	Cont.	Exp.	Cont.
	NO. OF CASES	64	72	23	16	84	91	92	90	263	269
Recall Test Gain—Picture-Unit Items	Mean	81.66	72.50	159.50	81.50	108.54	81.82	109.70	93.98	106.54	84.54
	S.D.Dist.	34.28	42.38	27.50	16.85	32.18	23.58	41.35	35.14	49.12	30.96
	S.D.M.	4.29	5.00	5.73	4.21	3.51	2.47	4.31	3.70	3.03	1.89
	Diff.Means	9.16		78.00		26.72		15.72		22.00	
	C.R.	1.39		10.97		6.23		2.77		6.16	
	% Sup.	12.6		95.7		32.6		16.7		26.0	
Recall Test Gain—Non-Picture Items	Mean	22.58	21.90	49.66	28.26	32.26	26.74	25.70	29.10	29.14	26.30
	S.D.Dist.	12.16	16.94	10.92	13.96	15.21	12.23	14.38	13.40	15.72	14.44
	S.D.M.	1.52	2.00	2.28	3.49	1.66	1.28	1.50	1.41	.97	.88
	Diff.Means	.68		21.40		5.52			3.40	2.84	
	C.R.	.27		5.13		2.63			1.66	2.17	
	% Sup.	3.1		75.7		20.6			13.2	10.8	
Per Cent Retention on Recall Test from Final Test	Mean	76.49	80.03	87.95	79.07	80.15	73.88	75.98	81.83	78.35	81.02
	S.D.Dist.	20.22	22.98	6.09	14.25	15.63	12.27	17.28	16.47	18.09	18.06
	S.D.M.	2.55	2.73	1.30	3.56	1.71	1.29	1.80	1.74	1.12	1.13
	Diff.Means		3.54	8.88		6.27			5.85		2.67
	C.R.		.95	2.34		2.93			2.34		1.68
	% Sup.		4.6	11.2		8.5			7.7		3.4

TABLE M

TOTAL SCIENCE TEST RESULTS FOR GROUPS OF BELOW AVERAGE AND
ABOVE AVERAGE INTELLIGENCE FOR COMBINED CITIES

| | | LOW I.Q. GROUP (BELOW 90) | | HIGH I.Q. GROUP (ABOVE 110) | |
		Experimental	Control	Experimental	Control
NUMBER OF CASES		50	63	130	110
Chronological Ages (In Months)	Med.	140.17	141.39	123.03	124.81
	Mean	141.50	142.88	122.72	124.08
	Q.	8.40	6.83	3.35	2.67
	S.D.$_{Dist.}$	14.24	11.09	5.65	5.33
	S.D.$_{M.}$	2.02	1.40	.50	.51
	Diff.$_{Means}$		1.38		1.36
	C.R.		.56		1.92
	% Sup.		1.0		1.1
Intelligence Quotient	Med.	84.30	82.80	118.84	118.50
	Mean	81.20	80.70	121.38	122.30
	Q.	5.77	5.78	5.88	7.62
	S.D.$_{Dist.}$	7.87	7.50	10.09	10.76
	S.D.$_{M.}$	1.11	.94	.89	1.03
	Diff.$_{Means}$		.49		.92
	C.R.		.34		.68
	% Sup.		0.6		0.8
Initial Test	Med.	77.50	78.50	104.50	115.50
	Mean	79.20	81.34	110.35	115.25
	Q.	11.46	15.20	17.54	17.35
	S.D.$_{Dist.}$	20.50	22.28	30.24	24.50
	S.D.$_{M.}$	2.90	2.81	2.65	2.34
	Diff.$_{Means}$		2.12		4.90
	C.R.		.52		1.39
	% Sup.		0.7		4.4
Gains over Initial Test	Med.	136.50	81.17	201.64	173.07
	Mean	132.82	96.82	198.34	173.30
	Q.	55.83	28.13	27.30	28.08
	S.D.$_{Dist.}$	59.99	45.54	39.46	43.51
	S.D.$_{M.}$	8.49	5.74	3.46	4.15
	Diff.$_{Means}$		36.00		25.04
	C.R.		3.51		4.64
	% Sup.		37.2		14.5
Gains— Picture-Unit Items	Mean	80.30	48.10	116.95	86.30
	S.D.$_{Dist.}$	38.20	23.75	26.30	24.40
	S.D.$_{M.}$	5.40	2.99	2.31	2.33
	Diff.$_{Means}$		32.20		30.65
	C.R.		5.22		9.34
	% Sup.		66.9		35.5
Gains— Non-Picture Items	Mean	50.22	49.62	83.30	88.06
	S.D.$_{Dist.}$	24.88	25.16	20.08	22.00
	S.D.$_{M.}$	3.52	3.17	1.76	2.10
	Diff.$_{Means}$		.60		4.76
	C.R.		.13		1.74
	% Sup.		1.2		5.7

TABLE N

TOTAL MUSIC TEST RESULTS FOR GROUPS OF BELOW AVERAGE AND
ABOVE AVERAGE INTELLIGENCE FOR CITIES A–D COMBINED

| | | LOW I.Q. GROUP (BELOW 90) | | HIGH I.Q. GROUP (ABOVE 110) | |
		Experimental	Control	Experimental	Control
NUMBER OF CASES		67	46	54	63
Intelligence	Med.	82.6	85.09	116.5	116.19
Quotient	Mean	81.85	84.11	118.20	117.41
	Q.	3.86	2.68	3.13	2.93
	S.D.$_{Dist.}$	4.52	4.00	5.29	4.80
	S.D.$_{M.}$	.55	.59	.72	.60
	Diff.$_{Means}$		2.26		.79
	C.R.		2.79		.84
	% Sup.		2.8		0.7
Initial Test	Med.	88.36	100.17	149.5	165.00
	Mean	96.78	105.50	153.50	169.26
	Q.	19.94	23.67	24.8	26.42
	S.D.$_{Dist.}$	33.44	30.32	35.04	44.48
	S.D.$_{M.}$	4.09	4.47	4.77	5.60
	Diff.$_{Means}$		8.72		15.76
	C.R.		1.44		2.14
	% Sup.		9.0		10.3
Gains over	Med.	147.67	103.50	181.00	140.38
Initial Test	Mean	153.60	111.80	185.40	140.90
	Q.	38.43	32.57	38.13	20.42
	S.D.$_{Dist.}$	49.20	38.20	48.50	35.53
	S.D.$_{M.}$	6.01	5.63	6.60	4.48
	Diff.$_{Means}$	41.80		44.50	
	C.R.	5.07		5.58	
	% Sup.	37.4		31.6	
Gains—	Mean	123.10	86.15	141.10	103.81
Picture-Unit	S.D.$_{Dist.}$	37.40	29.60	36.85	22.10
Items	S.D.$_{M.}$	4.57	4.36	5.01	2.78
	Diff.$_{Means}$	36.95		37.29	
	C.R.	5.85		6.51	
	% Sup.	42.9		35.9	
Gains—	Mean	31.66	28.76	44.06	33.64
Non-Picture	S.D.$_{Dist.}$	15.72	12.14	17.54	13.22
Items	S.D.$_{M.}$	1.92	1.79	2.39	1.67
	Diff.$_{Means}$	2.90		10.42	
	C.R.	1.11		3.57	
	% Sup.	10.1		31.0	